DANGER • DANGER • DANGER • DANGER • DANGER • DANGER • DANGER • DANGER • DANGER • DANGER • DANGER • DANGER • DANGER • DANGER • D

Brimming with creative inspiration, how-to projects, and useful information to enrich your everyday life, Quarto Knows is a favorite destination for those pursuing their interests and passions. Visit our site and dig deeper with our books into your area of interest: Quarto Creates, Quarto Cooks, Quarto Homes, Quarto Lives, Quarto Drives, Quarto Explores, Quarto Gifts, or Quarto Kids.

First published in 2018 by Voyageur Press, an imprint of The Quarto Group, 401 Second Avenue North, Suite 310, Minneapolis, MN 55401 USA.
T (612) 344-8100 F (612) 344-8692 www.QuartoKnows.com

Voyageur Press titles are also available at discount for retail, wholesale, promotional, and bulk purchase. For details, contact the Special Sales Manager by email at specialsales@quarto.com or by mail at The Quarto Group, Attn: Special Sales Manager, 401 Second Avenue North, Suite 310, Minneapolis, MN 55401 USA.

10 9 8 7 6 5 4 3 2 1

ISBN: 978-0-7603-5417-9

Library of Congress Cataloging-in-Publication Data

Names: Witzel, Michael Karl, 1960- author.
Title: Strange 66 : myth, mystery, mayhem, and other weirdness on Route 66 / Michael Karl Witzel.
Other titles: Strange sixty-six
Description: Minneapolis, Minnesota : Voyageur Press, an imprint of The Quarto Group, 2018.
Identifiers: LCCN 2018008592 | ISBN 9780760354179 (plc)
Subjects: LCSH: United States Highway 66. | Cultural landscapes--West (U.S.)
Classification: LCC HE356.U55 W585 2018 | DDC 917.804/34--dc23
LC record available at https://lccn.loc.gov/2018008592

Acquiring Editor: Dennis Pernu
Project Manager: Alyssa Bluhm
Art Direction and Cover Design: Cindy Samargia Laun
Page Design: Mind Spark Creative
Page Layout: Rebecca Pagel

On the front and back cover: Troy Paiva
On the endpapers: Vitezslav Valka/SkillUp/Shutterstock.com
On the frontis: 2Khans Photo Arts/Shutterstock.com

Printed in China

MYTH, MYSTERY, MAYHEM, AND OTHER WEIRDNESS ON ROUTE 66

MICHAEL KARL WITZEL

VOYAGEUR
PRESS

CONTENTS

This book is dedicated to all American Indian tribes,
the original and indigenous inhabitants of the Americas, survivors
of what might very well be the first American Holocaust.

INTRODUCTION

Back in the 1980s, while traveling across the country on the way to start a new contract engineering assignment, my wife and I found ourselves traveling in separate cars. She was driving in her vehicle alone, and I was pulling my own car with a rented moving van. We were driving on old Route 66 into California, and then heading north to Seattle.

This was long before the advent of cell phones and texting, so we had no practical way to contact each other if we were separated. The only plan of action was to call one of our parents long-distance from a payphone, check in with our general location, and tell them that we were safe.

The first clue that this was destined to be no ordinary trip was while traversing the Mojave Desert, heading straight into the setting sun. With our maps marked to Needles, the Joshua trees provided otherworldly set dressing for a moonlit night. But after crossing the Texas panhandle and New Mexico, we were both overly tired. Time and space seemed distorted. In an effort to rejuvenate, we stopped for gas and a cold drink.

A few minutes later, we were back on the road. Unfortunately, the minute I got up to highway speed, I thought I saw some sort of unidentified creature scurry across the pavement. I hit the brakes, and my drink spilled onto the floorboard. I had no choice but to stop to mop up the sticky mess. By the time I was finished, my wife's car had disappeared ahead . . . somewhere into the vanishing point. She was already barreling across that long expanse of desert, heading deep into the night.

I did what I could to catch up, racing across the hot pavement, sometimes topping speeds of ninety miles per hour. But it was getting late, and the ocean of highway ahead made my eyelids heavy. In the distance, eighteen-wheel behemoths bobbed up and down like so many whales, my headlights creating strange shapes when reflected off the diamond-shaped panels on the backs of their refrigerated reefers.

After a few hundred miles of monotonous driving, I could no longer discern if the light was moving away from me or getting closer. Suddenly, I entered a state of highway hypnosis, a place where one's senses can no longer be trusted. The dancing lights began to look like they were coming directly toward me and that an imminent collision was in order. I found myself slamming on the brakes and pulling over to the shoulder to avoid a collision. Of course, it was all in my imagination.

Eventually, I reached Needles, California, where I crossed the border and the agricultural checkpoint. "No, I don't have any fruit," I groaned. "But is there any chance you've seen my wife's car roll through here, a red Datsun 280Z?" Just about then I spied a group of very young children wheeling around on their bicycles. Mind you, it was 10:30 at night. I thought it was odd that kids would be allowed out so late. What were these juvenile delinquents up to?

I began my cruise through town and scoured the motor courts with one eye, hoping to catch a glimpse of my wife's car. But all I saw were scenes evoking an Edward Hopper painting— shady characters leaning against walls, smoking cigarettes in the dark, eyeballing me as if to say, "Whadda you want?" Nevertheless, my diligence paid off: a few minutes later, I found her car parked in the lot of a roadside motor court. I pulled in and there was my wife under the neon, waiting.

We checked into the hotel and discovered that the layout was disturbingly similar to the Bates Motel portrayed in the film *Psycho*, with parking directly outside each room. Things got even more strange when the desk clerk assigned us the room next to the office (just like Norman Bates did in the movie)! Even my wife was spooked. After we got settled, we made a close inspection of the walls and pictures to reassure ourselves that there were no peepholes.

That night, my dreams were mixed with the strange lights I had almost collided with out on the highway; those weird kids who were most likely criminals in the making, out there trying to break into my truck; the shady vagrants with nothing to do; and the creepy hotel clerk who most likely had his poor dead mother stored away in a broom closet. It was a fitful sleep, interrupted by strange noises and the urge to peer out the window to verify that everything was all right.

The next morning, I went out to check on my truck, fully expecting smashed windows and a body stripped bare to the chassis. But the sky was blue and birds were singing. In the sunlight of a new day, the ominous back-alley shadows of the night before had evaporated.

As I added sugar and cream to my diner coffee, I pondered the lives that run parallel to our own yet seem so foreign to us. I've made many high-mileage road trips before, but this was the first time I realized we're all just visitors in the realities of others. Yes, there exists another part of the road that most people never experience, a so-called unseen dimension. As we crisscross the country, we see only brief excerpts, highlights from a greater story yet untold.

Bottom line: Yes, Virginia, there is a boogey-man, hobgoblin, or evil clown waiting to sink his fangs into your neck when the lights go out. Like it or not, criminals, murderers, and other miscreants occupy the road too, scurrying underneath that threadbare carpet like cockroaches. Hideous creatures are hiding in the wall, scrabbling through the insulation like rats. There's a monster beneath the bed waiting to steal your breath— hiding under the covers won't save you.

With all these images spinning in my head, I promised myself that for the rest of the trip, I would take off my rose-colored glasses and pull down my protective defenses for a change. Like the audience waiting for the next shock in a horror movie, I wanted to witness the hidden underbelly of Highway 66 that most people miss. I wanted to experience that rollercoaster thrill you get in the pit of your stomach when something unexpectedly pops out to scare and amaze you.

All I had to do was get in my vehicle, hit the gas, and be patient. Before long, the next event would unfold right before my eyes, allowing me— for a brief moment—to capture a glimpse of the myth, mystery, mayhem, and other weirdness often found along the forgotten miles of the strange highway numbered 66.

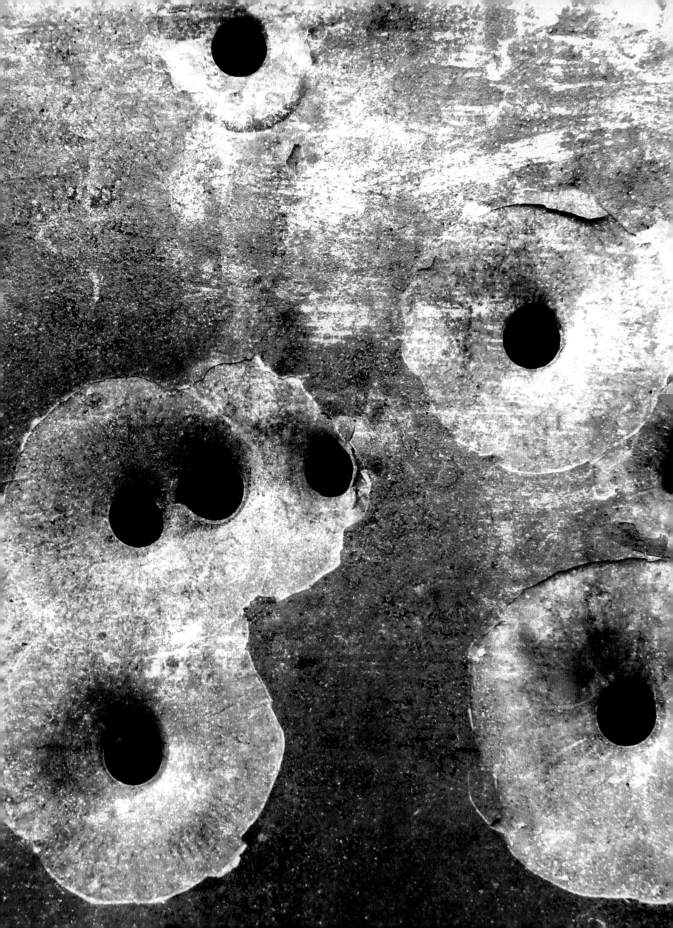

THERE'S A KILLER ON THE ROAD

There's a Killer on the Road retrieves the rap sheet of murder and mayhem from the archives of highway history and shines a bright light on the most notorious crimes and criminals that darkened the roadsides of the old Route 66. America's so-called "Mother Road" at one time may have been a nurturing road for innocents seeking to flee the poverty of the Dust Bowl for a new life out west, but it also became a road of escape (and opportunity) for bootleggers, robbers, murderers, and others addicted to the roadside noir of America's Main Street.

1.
AL CAPONE ON 66

CHICAGO AND CICERO, ILLINOIS

During his heyday, Capone earned the nickname "Snorky," a term many people of the age used to describe a sharp dresser.

Al "Scarface" Capone was known as many things: gangster, mobster, criminal, lawbreaker, bouncer, bootlegger, racketeer, tax-evader, modern-day Robin Hood, and "Public Enemy Number One." What isn't widely known is that at one time he reigned as the de facto king of the Route 66 town of Cicero, Illinois—or "Caponeville," as some called it.

It all started in New York City, in a section of lower Manhattan known as Five Points, a slum where nothing good ever came of anything. Capone grew up there and cut his eyeteeth on illegal activities, starting out as a small-time hoodlum in gangs such as the Bowery Boys. In his early twenties, he moved to Chicago, Illinois, to further his career. There he signed on as a bodyguard for Johnny Torrio and under Torrio's tutelage worked as a bouncer at brothels.

After Torrio took a bullet in a retribution hit by the competing North Side Gang, he relinquished control of his operation to Capone. Only twenty-three years old, Al took charge of a sprawling distilling and sales operation that covered the entire Chicago area and stretched all the way to the Canadian border. Scarface was now at the top of the heap.

Eventually, the mayor of Chicago had enough and kicked Capone out, so he slithered off to do business in the nearby suburbs of Cicero, hoping to continue his bootlegging operation unimpeded. Naturally, he used his illicit earnings to grease the wheels of the local government, once boasting, "Graft is a byword in American life today. . . . The honest lawmakers of any city can be counted on your fingers."

In 1924, when someone ran against his shill, Mayor Joseph Klenha, Capone unleashed his fury on the opposing candidate. Henchmen shot up the Democratic candidate's office and strong-arm men known as "sluggers" beat up campaigners. Outside polling facilities, voters were intimidated by Capone's thugs and quizzed about their allegiance. Anyone voting the Democratic ticket was hit with a billy club, kicked down the street, or knee-capped.

ABOVE LEFT: Capone's getaway cars copied the colors of police cruisers; others were armored to protect him from flying lead. This model had a removable back window.

ABOVE RIGHT: Al Capone was never sent away to pay for his most egregious crimes. He served hard time for tax evasion, the only real crime that the authorities could make stick.

BELOW: Despite his illegal activities, Capone endeared himself to the local populace by sponsoring soup kitchens and other charitable enterprises.

In 1929, Capone was arrested for carrying an unlicensed .38-caliber revolver outside of a movie theater in Pennsylvania. He served a one-year sentence in near luxury.

"Bullets Fly in Cicero on Election Eve," read the *Chicago Tribune* headline. As it happened, brothers Frank and Ralph Capone led a motorcade of shooters on a mission of preelection mayhem. Their orders? Kidnap election workers or literally punch them out in the streets. Stanley Stankievitch was the first to get nabbed. According to the paper, he was "blindfolded, carried to a basement, and held prisoner until eight o'clock last night." A total of twenty men were taken against their will, strong-armed to another side of town, and then chained to the pipes and posts in the basement of a city plumbing shop.

As the sun went down, election officials sent out an urgent call for help: Cicero was in a state of complete and total anarchy! The response from law enforcement was quick, and a small army of seventy Chicago cops and five squads of detectives from a nearby bureau rolled into Cicero on Route 66. With Cicero in tatters, the cavalry tried their best to restore law and order. When they stopped to investigate what three gunmen were up to near 22nd Street and Cicero Avenue, bullets cut the air. One of the men shot at the detectives, but he missed. The detectives soon returned fire with equal force, killing the man on the spot. The man turned out to be Al's brother, Frank Capone.

When the election fighting concluded, Scarface emerged from the shadows and claimed victory. Cicero was now in his back pocket. Feeling quite at home, he moved into the top three floors of the Hawthorne Hotel and turned the place into his criminal headquarters. He also bought a handful of local properties, the most memorable being the "party house" on South Austin Boulevard that he kept stocked with plenty of food, booze, and broads.

All the Cicero properties were near Route 66, which gave Capone and his criminal associates an easy path both in and out of Chicago. The road cut a southwesterly path through the grid of surface streets and provided the most direct way to access the many business concerns they juggled. Whether it was one of his bootleg delivery trucks or getaway cars painted to copy the colors of cop cars, Route 66 became just another facet of Al Capone's illegal businesses.

"If you smell gunpowder, then you're in Cicero" was the saying of the day. During the reign of King Capone, the once-sleepy bedroom community of Chicago was a hotbed of criminal activity and a venue for some of the most notorious mob crimes ever committed in the United States.

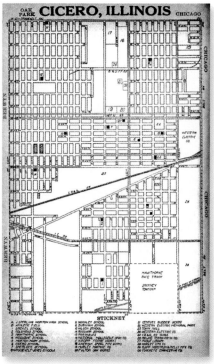

The Thompson submachine gun reduced a half dozen armed men to a crumpled pile of blood and guts in a matter of seconds, without having to reload.

TOP: The town of Cicero was close enough to Chicago for Al Capone and his gang to enjoy "family life" and commute to work (on Route 66).

ABOVE: Bootlegging may not have been the most heinous of crimes, but it was the damage that occurred to the innocent bystander that garnered the most attention.

2.

JESSE JAMES'S HIDEOUT CAVE

MERAMEC, MISSOURI

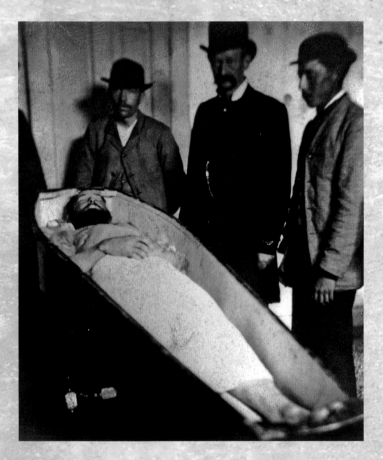

After Jesse James was captured and killed, the authorities displayed his body (resting comfortably in a plain wooden coffin) to the general public.

Jesse Woodson James wasn't always an outlaw. He was born in 1847 in Clay County, Missouri, a location known as "Little Dixie" due to the high concentration of settlers from Kentucky and Tennessee who lived there. During the American Civil War, his family sided with the Confederates and joined other local fighters who engaged in guerilla warfare, a style of fighting that relied on a deadly mix of ambush, sabotage, and hit-and-run raids.

When he was only sixteen, he followed the lead of his brother Frank and became a secessionist "bushwhacker," doing all that he could do to cripple the Union forces. With that aim, he joined up with a band of irregulars led by William C. Quantrill, a former drifter, school teacher, and cattle rustler. In 1863, the group discovered that Union troops had established a secret munitions powder mill at the Saltpeter Cave, a naturally formed cavern on the Meramec River, near Stanton, Missouri.

Despite the fact that pre-Columbian artifacts have been found in the caverns (some American Indians consider it the home of their god), historical accounts cite that a French miner by the name of Renault was the first to "discover" the secluded cave system in 1742. Unfortunately, spelunkers of the age—armed only with kerosene lanterns and handheld torches—were only

MERAMEC CAVERNS

U.S. 66 STANTON, MO.

MERAMEC CAVERNS

"The 5-Story Wonder Cave" **STANTON, MO.** Highway 66

able to behold a small percentage of the fantastic mineral formations that lined the caverns.

Without electrification and the ability to illuminate this underground wonderland, there was scant interest in promoting and popularizing the site as a natural wonder or tourist attraction. In the nineteenth century, the caves provided a ready supply of potassium nitrate, also known as saltpeter. Used as an oxidizer in the formula for making gunpowder, it was an indispensable resource for the advancing Union Army.

Strangely, Union forces didn't protect this asset adequately enough. When Quantrill and his small band of horseback raiders stumbled upon the operation in the mid-1860s, they met with little resistance and summarily destroyed the mill's production equipment and quickly moved on to their next conquest.

$500 REWARD

For the Arrest and Conviction of

JESSE JAMES

St. Louis Midland Railroad

TOP: To promote the caverns, Lester Dill created a rectangular sign that was attached to the bumper of a car with wires—the forerunner to the modern bumper sticker.

ABOVE RIGHT: Once upon a time, Jesse James was one of the most wanted men in America. At one point, the Saint Louis Midland Railway offered a bounty of $500.

RIGHT: Bob Ford's New Model No. 3 single-action .44-caliber Smith & Wesson revolver, also known as "the gun that killed Jesse James," once sold at auction for $350,000.

ABOVE: Beneath the rolling hills of Missouri's Meramec Valley, a 4.6-mile complex of limestone mineral formations awaits inside an interconnected cave system.

But the story of Saltpeter Cave didn't end there. As legend later revealed, the caves made more than a big impression on young Jesse James. What young man wouldn't be fascinated by an underground cave system that would make a great hideout when you ran away from home? It would be the perfect place to elude anyone who might be in hot pursuit.

And as history tells it, a place to hide out was soon something that the James brothers desperately needed. In September, Jesse and his brother Frank took part in the brutal Centralia Massacre in Missouri. There, Quantrill and his raiders killed twenty-two unarmed Union soldiers returning home by train. The raiders shot the men and viciously scalped the victims and dismembered some of the bodies.

When the 39th Missouri Infantry Regiment led by Major A. V. E. Johnston pursued the ambushers, their muzzleloader rifles proved no match for the gang's rapid-fire six-shooters. There were 147 Union soldiers when it began; when it was over, only 24 survived. Major Johnston was among the dead, and Jesse was part of the group that killed him—a fact that would not soon be forgotten by the army.

The Union forced the James family out of Clay County and instructed them to relocate South, across Union lines. But they moved to Nebraska instead, where Jesse continued to burnish his brand. In 1874, he joined up with the James-Younger gang and assisted with the strong-arm robbery of the Little Rock Express. The train was traveling from Saint Louis, Missouri, to Little Rock, Arkansas, when it was ambushed and robbed in a little town called Gads Hill.

It didn't take long before a posse was organized to hunt down James and his cohorts. By all accounts, they pursued the outlaws on horseback some seventy-five miles to the northeast, tracking them to the present-day site known as Meramec Caverns.

Rather than rush into the dark caverns and face the barrel of a gun, the posse decided to wait it out until the gang ran out of food. Three days passed and no one emerged from the cave. Finally, they went inside but found only horses. And so began the local legend: James and company escaped through a little-known back door and swam through a shallow underground river that connected to the Meramec River.

ABOVE LEFT: Meramec Caverns is one of Missouri's top tourist attractions along old Route 66, its history colored by the amazing tale of how Jesse James eluded the law.

ABOVE RIGHT: Inside the caverns, promotional figures take the Jesses James "outlaw hideout" theme to the next level, even though the supposed escape route was never retraced.

OPPOSITE: Natural rock formations are wonderful, but a connection with an American legend is the best promotion a tourist trap could hope for, especially if the legend is Jesse James.

3.
BONNIE AND CLYDE SHOOTOUT

JOPLIN, MISSOURI

Bonnie Elizabeth Parker and Clyde Chestnut Barrow roamed the central states with their gang during the Great Depression, robbing folks and killing a few.

Anyone interested in the morbid side of criminal history no doubt has seen the photograph of Bonnie and Clyde's getaway car riddled with hundreds of bullet holes, a coffin on wheels for the larcenous duo when they met their end. But they had many other less publicized shootouts in their career, one of which entered the history books right off old 66 in Joplin, Missouri.

The incident took place a short while after Buck Barrow was granted a pardon on March 22, 1933, and released from prison. With wife Blanche in tow, he headed for Joplin and shacked up with his brother, Clyde Barrow, and Bonnie Parker, along with a miscreant and childhood friend by the name of William Daniel Jones. Their temporary hideout was an upstairs apartment located at 3347½ Oakridge Drive. It was hardly glamorous, but it was safe from the cops. For a time, the group could come and go as they pleased.

Buck and Blanche were not there on a social call but rather for a last-ditch attempt at intervention. The heat was on Clyde big time, and they were hoping that they could convince him to surrender to the cops before things went completely south. But Clyde wasn't ready to give up his freewheeling life of crime. In fact, Buck soon joined him in several armed robberies.

Maintaining a low profile proved easier said than done for the group. Possibly hyped up on adrenaline from the local stickups, they proceeded to hold loud, alcohol-fueled card games well into the wee

hours of the morning. "We bought a case of beer a day," Blanche later told the authorities. The drunken posse created all kinds of commotion when they came and went, disturbing neighbors to no end.

The partying reached a crescendo when Clyde accidentally discharged his rifle while cleaning it in the apartment. By this time, the neighbors were so spooked by the raucous behavior that no one dared even confront the rabble. Finally, one person decided that enough was enough and called in a report to the Joplin Police Department.

Believing a gang of bootleggers was holed up in the rock-faced structure, the cops put together a five-man force and headed over to the apartment in two cars to make what they thought would be some easy arrests. What ensued on April 13, 1933, was a complete surprise to all parties involved. As the cops stormed the flat, Clyde stayed true to his reputation for being cool under fire. Without hesitation, he followed Jones and Buck in calmly retrieving their handguns and laid down a volley of bullets that quickly killed Detective Harry McGinnis and fatally wounded Constable J. W. Harryman.

As the criminal cast of characters scrambled to exit, bullets flew everywhere. Jones caught some lead in his side, but Clyde managed to escape injury when one of his coat buttons deflected a bullet. Buck was grazed by a slug that ricocheted off a wall. To hasten the move to

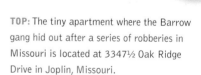

TOP: The tiny apartment where the Barrow gang hid out after a series of robberies in Missouri is located at 3347½ Oak Ridge Drive in Joplin, Missouri.

ABOVE: A submachine gun wasn't the type of weapon that you could flash in public. The most well-heeled criminals chose to transport and disguise their weapons in stylish cases.

their car, Bonnie Parker unleashed a fury of cover fire from her rifle. In the nick of time, highway patrol Sergeant G. B. Kahler took cover behind a large oak tree as .30-caliber bullets shredded the other side, ripping wood splinters directly into his face.

By no small miracle, and with superior firepower, the gang managed to pull away in their vehicle, pulling Blanche Barrow up onto the running board and into the passenger compartment as they sped away. Unfazed by the mayhem, she had been in the street calmly

Joplin, Missouri, had a bad reputation long before the Barrow gang rolled into town. At the turn of the century, it was a ragtag boomtown riddled with vice.

WANTED FOR MURDER
JOPLIN, MISSOURI

F.P.C.29 - MO. 9
26 U 00 6

CLYDE CHAMPION BARROW, age 24, 5'7", 130#, hair dark brown and wavy, eyes hazel, light complexion, home West Dallas, Texas. This man killed Detective Harry McGinnis and Constable J.W. Harryman in this city, April 13, 1933.

BONNIE PARKER CLYDE BARROW   CLYDE BARROW

This man is dangerous and is known to have committed the following murders: Howard Hall, Sherman, Texas; J.N.Bucher, Hillsboro, Texas; a deputy sheriff at Atoka, Okla; deputy sheriff at West Dallas, Texas; also a man at Belden, Texas.

The above photos are kodaks taken by Barrow and his companions in various poses, and we believe they are better for identification than regular police pictures.

Wire or write any information to the

Police Department.

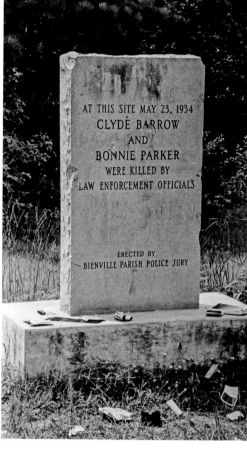

chasing down her dog, Snow Ball. Somehow, the gang sped out of town on 66 and onto back roads, avoiding capture.

They left behind most of their belongings, some of which provided revealing insight into their lives. Police found a large arsenal of weapons, of course, but what they didn't expect was a handwritten poem by Bonnie, along with a camera and several rolls of undeveloped film.

The *Joplin Globe* later processed the negatives and produced the now infamous photographs that showcased the gang. Scenes of Barrow, Parker, and Jones fooling around and pointing guns at each other provided a rare glimpse into the lives of the troupe. One photo of Parker holding a pistol in one hand while clenching a cigar in her teeth caught the public's imagination like no other. The "Barrow Gang" was loose on Route 66 . . . and coming soon to a town near you!

ABOVE LEFT: After the police raided Bonnie and Clyde's small hideout in Joplin, they found a camera with undeveloped film, a find that later became a treasure trove.

ABOVE RIGHT: In a withering salvo of bullets issued by a posse of four Texas officers, Clyde Barrow and Bonnie Parker were killed on a rural Louisiana road on May 23, 1934.

4.
GALENA'S BLOODY MADAM

GALENA, KANSAS

The Kansas Murder Bordello conjures up the base fears of every traveler: being strangled while you sleep or hacked up with an axe by a crazed psychopath.

During the early 1890s, the Galena Mining Company built a small home seven miles west of Joplin, Missouri, in the city of Galena, Kansas. The funny thing is, the builders didn't intend to use it as a rental or to sell it for profit; its sole purpose was as a brothel for employees. In those days, local mining concerns were quite wealthy, and the employer apparently was looking for ways to keep its employees from jumping ship.

For years, the brothel was run by the Staffleback family, although some reports say that that they didn't live in the home themselves. "Ma" Staffleback and her sons, including George, ran the brothel's day-to-day operations and turned it into a favorite respite along Highway 66. However, what customers who stopped there during those years didn't realize was that this pleasure palace was more like a house of horrors. As it turns out, some of the miners who stayed there lost all their money . . . and their lives. Nearby mining shafts provided places to dump the bodies of the murdered victims.

The September 15, 1897, issue of the *Chicago Tribune* shared with its readers the story of how Cora, George Staffleback's wife at the time, confessed to authorities that she had seen Ma rob, murder,

When Galena and its brothels were in full swing, motorcars like this 1924 Franklin plied the local roadways and later Route 66.

and then dump a man into a mining tunnel. That unfortunate man was Frank Galbraith, whose body was later found bloated and floating in the subterranean chamber just a few miles from Staffleback home.

Soon more incriminating information leaked out that Ma and her boys had robbed and murdered others. Two women living at the bordello had witnessed the crimes but were told to keep their traps shut. That might have been the end of it had not one of the ladies had a heated argument with Mike Staffleback (another of Ma's sons) a few days later and threatened to leave the house.

There was no way that Mike Staffleback could be sure that she wouldn't go to the authorities, so he decided to snuff her out, which he did in front of one of his other brothers and the other woman. The other woman tried in vain to help her friend, but she was unable to overpower Staffleback, and yet another victim was added to the list of those dispatched to an early death.

Estimates have it that, over the years, as many as fifty people were robbed and killed at the bordello. However, the family, including the

With only 13.2 miles of roadway joining Missouri and Oklahoma, Kansas Route 66 has a lot of catching up to do when it comes to highway legends.

RIGHT: An ominous hand-carved statue depicting a murder of crows became part of the restoration effort when the Galena, Kansas, murder bordello was recently updated.

BELOW: In 2013, Russ Keeler (After Midnight Paranormal Investigations) persuaded the co-owners of the 1890s Staffleback House to restore it. Guided tours were planned.

Staffleback mother, father, and two of the sons, were only officially charged with Galbraith's murder. Nevertheless, Ma Staffleback earned the nickname "Galena's Bloody Madam" and died in 1909 while incarcerated for the heinous crime.

Curiously enough, the building later was used for a short while as a nursing home, with one of the rooms reserved for the temporary storage of bodies when residents passed away.

Perhaps not surprisingly, visitors have reported experiencing paranormal activity there since the home was first renovated and reopened in 2013, citing a long list of unusual occurrences: rattling doors, cold spots, beds moving away from the wall, electrical disturbances, orb manifestations, slamming doors, and rocking chairs that move back and forth all by themselves.

Even so, there are visitors a plenty. Tours once were conducted regularly at "Galena's Murder Bordello," including some led by well-known paranormal experts. The former house of ill repute continues to draw a gaggle of sightseers eager to get their paranormal kicks on Route 66. Currently, the residence houses an antique shop.

It's a place that those passing by won't easily miss. With a style more suited to the Munsters than an ordinary home, the exterior features sullen hues of black and gray. In the yard, a chainsaw sculpture of nine crows takes a place of prominence (a group of crows is called a "murder," of course). A large stained-glass window of a naked woman provides a less-than-subtle reminder of the building's sordid past.

Like so many fighting birds, historians have stirred up a cloud of controversy regarding the murders, the house, and the Staffleback family. Some challenge where the dastardly deeds were committed; others question how many people died. But the public seems to care less about the details than about the legend. As the controversies swirl around the murderous truth, so too does the interest that people have in seeing and learning about this famous erstwhile serial-killer brothel on Route 66.

ABOVE RIGHT: "Old Nancy Staffleback" drew a sentence of twenty-one years in the infamous 1897 trial for miner Galbraith's murder.

RIGHT: Whether or not the Staffleback house is part of the "four room log cabin" described in this article is inconsequential. The murders of innocent people did, in fact, happen.

OLD NANCY STAFFLEBACK.

MURDER AS A TRADE

Kansas Has a Rival for the Bender Family.

STORY OF MANY CRIMES.

Horrible Confession of Mrs. George Staffelback.

MEN MURDERED FOR MONEY.

Joplin, Mo., Sept. 14.—[Special.]—Not since the horrible crimes of the Bender family were revealed has southeastern Kansas been so excited and so bent upon vengeance until the bloody butcheries committed by the Staffleback family at Galena were brought to light by the confession of Cora Staffleback yesterday, and George Staffleback on the witness stand at Columbus to-day.

When upon trial for the murder of Frank Galbreath, whose body was found floating in an old abandoned mining shaft near the Staffleback home last July, Cora Staffleback weakened and told all she knew about the murder of Galbreath and others whom the family had killed.

George Staffleback, Cora's husband, without knowing what his wife had revealed, made a similar confession. They said that Galbreath, who had been murdered and robbed by the Staffleback boys and their mother was not the only person they had murdered, but that an Italian peddler, whose name they did not know, had been killed and robbed about two years ago, and his body thrown in an old abandoned mining shaft about forty yards from the Staffleback house.

At that time Mrs. Charles Wilson, mother of the Staffleback boys, kept a questionable resort in the four-room log cabin where these crimes were committed. Two girls, whose names George Staffleback could not give, were living there at the time, and saw the peddler murdered.

5.
THE GREENLEASE KIDNAPPING

SAINT LOUIS, MISSOURI

CORAL COURT
Ultra-Modern
One of the finest
in the Mid-West
on U. S. Highway 66
City Route, one mile
west of City Limits,
three miles east of
intersection of By Pass.
Highways #61, 66, 67
and 77

70 rooms, tile cottages
with private tile bath
in each room.
Hot and cold water
porter and maid service
—Beauty Rest Spring
and mattresses—
Hot Water Radiant
Heat—24 Hour Service
7755 Watson Road
(Highway 66)
St. Louis 19, Mo.

WOODLAND 2-5786

The Coral Court Motel used to be the most modern accommodations that you could find anywhere on Route 66, featuring Beauty Rest Spring and Mattresses.

For those fascinated by true crime stories that have a connection to Route 66, the Greenlease kidnapping is a sad case with more than its share of humanity's malevolent and greedy sides. It was a story that rocked the nation, igniting headlines from coast to coast. How it unfolded remains shocking even by today's standards and still leaves people wondering about the parts unsolved.

The story begins on September 28, 1953, with a knock at the door of Notre Dame de Sion, an exclusive private school in Kansas City, Missouri. The woman at the door told the nun that she was the aunt of Bobby Greenlease, a six-year-old student there. The boy's mother had suffered a serious heart attack, the woman said, and she was there to retrieve him. Without question, the nun rushed to get the boy, who went right to the woman without the slightest indication that she might be a stranger. The lady grabbed hold of the boy's hand and hastily rushed him into a waiting cab.

Unfortunately, the nun later learned that she had made a grave mistake. The boy's mother wasn't ill at all, and the "aunt" was an outright imposter. Her name was Bonnie Heady, and she had masterminded the kidnapping along with a man named Carl Austin

Hall as a scheme to make them wealthy. The boy's father was a well-to-do auto dealer in Kansas City—it would be child's play to extract a hefty ransom in exchange for the boy's return.

Shortly after the abduction, the duo began to send detailed ransom letters to the parents demanding $600,000 in small bills. They revealed that "the boy was doing fine, that he missed being home," and that "they would have their son back within 24 hours of them getting the cash." The parents followed the kidnapper's instructions and filled a duffel bag with cash. They left it at a predetermined location and waited by the phone, sure that they would get their little boy back.

But there was to be no such reunion. The horrible truth was that during the entire time the kidnappers were negotiating with the parents, the body of Bobby Greenlease was already cold—the couple had killed the boy after kidnapping him and buried him on Heady's property.

As soon as they received the ransom money, Heady and Hall fled to Saint Louis, which is where Route 66 enters the picture. As news of the heartless kidnappers broke coast to coast, the nation took interest. When the fugitives got wind of the press, they ditched their car and started using taxis. They rented out an apartment too, but it wasn't long before Hall, an alcoholic, hooked up with an ex-con and a prostitute.

He dumped Heady to shack up with the call girl and stayed at the Coral Court Motel, a stylish art deco motor court with a reputation as a "no-tell motel," located right off old 66 in Saint Louis. According to rumor, it was the kind of place where people could hide out from the cops. It was even suggested that the owner had mob ties and at one time ran a brothel in Saint Louis.

Austin successfully stayed on the lam for a couple of days without incident. Unfortunately, he was a little too free with his newly acquired stack of cash, and before long, a nosey taxi driver tipped off the cops

TOP: When Coral Court was demolished in 1995, one of the two-unit buildings was taken apart and reconstructed at the National Museum of Transportation in Saint Louis, Missouri.

ABOVE: The Villages at General Grant now occupy the space of the former Coral Court. The murder of little Bobby Greenlease and the related criminal activities have been long forgotten.

that something wasn't quite right at the Coral Court. The authorities picked up Austin, who freely blabbed about Heady's whereabouts. No heat-lamp questioning was even necessary. She was arrested for kidnapping the same day.

The ensuing FBI investigation led to the recovery of Bobby's decomposed body, as well as the pair's confessions and mounds of evidence. Their case went before the judge and within one hour of deliberations, the jury gave the couple the death sentence. The presiding magistrate was appalled at the crime, stating that "the verdict fits the evidence. It is the most cold-blooded, brutal murder I have ever tried." Justice moved faster than a speeding bullet in this case, and the couple was executed together in the gas chamber on December 18, 1953, just three months after the kidnapping.

ABOVE: Streamline Moderne architecture made the Coral Court building look fast. Individual garage units gave customers the ability to hide their cars, the ultimate in "no-tell" motel privacy.

LEFT: Watson Road used to be a quiet stretch of road along the old Route 66 Highway, but the local population increased dramatically, and the neighborhood slowly declined.

NXP12-10/12-ST.LOUIS,MO.:Carl Austin Hall and Mrs.Bonnie Heady confessed 10/12 here to
the kidnap-slaying of Bobby Greenlease,the FBI said.The Federal government has charged
them with violating Lindbergh law.B-11 and Mrs.Heady are pictured after their capture.
UNITED PRESS TELEPHOTO from files.   Jo.

ABOVE: Hall and Heady appeared well-dressed in their court appearances, reinforcing the old axiom that you can't tell a book—or, in this case, kidnapper—by its cover.

LEFT: The kidnappers confessed to the murder of Bobby Greenlease, but they provided no logical reason as to why the boy had to die in the cold-blooded manner that he did.

6.
THE MOSSER MASSACRE MURDERS

LUTHER, OKLAHOMA

In December 1950, Carl and Thelma Mosser were making the thousand-mile arc from Illinois to New Mexico with their three children. Their trip down 66 was uneventful until they reached Oklahoma on December 30. There, they decided to play Good Samaritan and stopped to assist a young man stranded on the roadside between Claremore and Tulsa. Little did they know that the hitchhiker they picked up was nowhere near helpless but a depraved predator who feasted on evil deeds and lived by the gun.

William Edward "Billy" Cook Jr., a droopy-eyed ne'er-do-well with a belligerent attitude (and former ward of the state with a rap sheet as long as your arm), regularly terrorized the citizens of Joplin, Missouri. After spending most of his youth in the Missouri State Penitentiary, Cook emerged with no morals or conscience and a degree in criminal behavior, bragging to his father the creed he would live by: "Easy dough. You've got to take it the hard way. I'm going to live by the gun and roam."

He had just driven in from Texas, where he bought a gun in El Paso. He first tested out the persuasive powers of his revolver in Lubbock, where he hitched a ride with a local mechanic, robbed him of his cash, and locked him in the trunk of his car. Fortunately, the man MacGyvered his way out and, by doing so, escaped certain death.

Carl Mosser wasn't as lucky as the previous victim. When Cook presented his .32-caliber snub nose and started barking orders, all he could do was comply. His first task was to drive. Over the next three days, Mosser and his terrorized family endured a mindless ride down America's Main Street, as Cook directed them through Oklahoma, Texas, New Mexico, Arkansas, and all the way back to Missouri. All they could do was to follow his directions while the gun-crazy Cook directed the car ride.

Seventy-two hours later, Cook grew tired of his road trip and brutally killed the entire brood (including the family dog), dumping the bodies in an abandoned mineshaft near his hometown of Joplin. If killing were an art form, this cross-country trip was his virtuoso performance.

Soon after Cook had ditched the Mossers' bullet-riddled car in Tulsa, the police were all over it, searching every bloodstained inch for clues. Much to their amazement, they found the receipt for Cook's gun. Within a matter of hours, he became the FBI's most wanted criminal.

Over the next twelve days, some two thousand law enforcement officers and citizens forming vigilante posses began scouring Route 66 and the Southwest, searching in vain for Cook. Newspapers had a field day with the story and glamorized the manhunt for the murderer with "HARD LUCK" tattooed on the fingers of his left hand, detailing the search progress as cops investigated every sighting that came across the wire.

Investigators quickly located the bodies of the five Mosser victims in their grisly grave. As the cops pulled the battered corpses of the family from the mineshaft, the search for a monster intensified.

Meanwhile, Cook kidnapped a sheriff's deputy in California and forced him to play chauffeur. For some inexplicable reason, the man was let go, unharmed. After this momentary display of mercy, the hellhounds controlling Cook's mind demanded even more blood, so

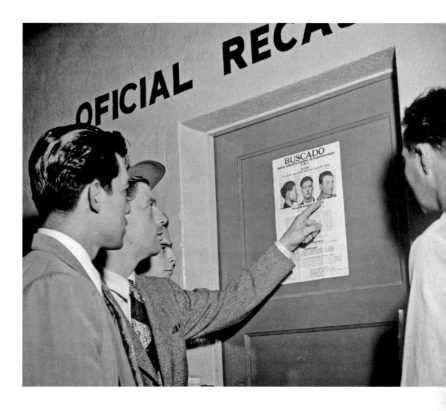

ABOVE: After Cook embarked on his heinous spree of murder and mayhem, the authorities mounted a manhunt of unprecedented size and scope, with wanted posters playing a big role.

OPPOSITE: A quick-thinking cop in Mexico spotted Billy Cook after he made his run across the border and apprehended him on the spot. Cook was quickly extradited back to the United States.

Cook's modus operandi included the old highwayman's trick of staging a car to appear he was a motorist in trouble, hoping a good Samaritan would stop.

he shot traveling salesman Robert Dewey execution style. By now, Cook knew that the FBI was hot on his trail, so he kidnapped a pair of hunters and made a last-ditch run for the Mexican border.

Fortunately, authorities in Santa Rosalía, Mexico, spotted Cook. There, a valiant police chief by the name of Luis Parra walked up to him and jerked the .32 revolver from his belt, slapping on the cuffs. By some accounts, when Cook was arrested he asked, "How high do they hang you in Oklahoma?" Believe it or not, he never found out.

To escape the death penalty, Cook pleaded guilty to the Mosser massacre and Oklahoma awarded him sixty years for each murder. But lethal justice was awaiting him in California, where he was tried for murder and sentenced to death. "I hate everyone's guts, and everyone hates my guts," Cook said. No one was listening: his filthy yap was finally silenced in 1952 when poison gas asphyxiated him in the state's death chamber.

ABOVE: Cook's worldview was as worn as the pavement depicted in this Route 66 highway marker. He decided to live his life by the gun and was eventually executed for his twisted convictions.

LEFT: A Missouri stretch of the old red asphalt-surfaced Route 66 as it might have looked during Billy Cook's murderous car drive that ended in the death of an entire family.

TOP FIVE

WEIRD
to go and
WEIRD
to do

1 2 3 4 5

AL CAPONE'S GRAVE

1400 South Wolf Road, Hillside, Illinois

Take a short hearse ride from Cicero to Hillside (to the northwest), and you'll find the final resting place of numerous local organized crime figures—the most notable being the gravesite of Al Capone himself. Check out the photo-engraved tombstones and the elaborate mausoleums.

JESSE JAMES WAX MUSEUM

I-44, Exit 230, Stanton, Missouri

Located just a pistol shot away from Meramec Caverns, this roadside attraction features lifelike wax figures, vignettes depicting the Jesse James home, the Civil War, and more. Artifacts direct from the James family are on display, including a vintage gun collection worth over $100,000.

JOLIET PRISON GATE

1125 Collins Street, Joliet, Illinois

The famed Joliet prison in Illinois is located just east of the Des Plaines River. Closed in 2002, the Joliet Correctional Center is best remembered for the opening sequence in the 1980s John Landis film *The Blues Brothers* and as the namesake of "Joliet" Jake Blues (John Belushi).

MURRAH BUILDING MEMORIAL

620 North Harvey Avenue, Oklahoma City, Oklahoma

The memorial for the victims of the Oklahoma City bombing is a somber destination that's a must-see when traveling the old Route 66 Highway through Oklahoma. "Come to Remember. Leave with Resolve." The 168 people killed are memorialized by the field of empty chairs.

AL CAPONE'S PARTY HOUSE

1600 Austin Boulevard, Cicero, Illinois

When Al Capone wasn't busy transporting bootleg spirits and fashioning cement overshoes for rivals, he liked to kick back at his Cicero "party house." Stocked with booze, broads, and food, it was a good distance away from his family home on Prairie Avenue (shown here).

MYSTERIES AND THE UNEXPLAINED

Tourists aren't the only ones who haunt Route 66. Many of the surviving towns, tourist attractions, and roadside businesses found along the old road host ghostly travelers from another dimension. These days, paranormal events are common occurrences along the lonely and forgotten paths of the old road. Mysteries and the Unexplained pulls back the shroud on the dark side of the highway to reveal an eerie, parallel world inhabited by ghosts, poltergeists, and things that go bump in the night.

1.
GHOST OF THE VANISHING HITCHHIKER

EL RENO, OKLAHOMA

From its early days as a collection of rutted wagon trails to its heyday of end-to-end pavement, Route 66 has played host to an energetic roster of roadside ghosts and apparitions. The highway seems to bring out the best—and worst—of people, whether in the land of the living or the afterlife. The funny thing is that these ghosts are almost always on the move, like the people who traveled the highway.

Consider a little-known spot in Albuquerque, New Mexico, where the spirit of La Llorona, the weeping woman, is said to wander a draining ditch called the Arroyo. She's searching for her lost children but will never find them. Apparently, the poor woman murdered her brood and is too crazy to realize what she has done. As penance, she's cursed to walk in that nether region between heaven and hell for eternity.

At the end of Menaul Boulevard in the foothills, visitors often hear sounds of screaming and dragged bodies. Legend has it that an old man with homicidal tendencies once lived in the caves atop the hill. Quite the player in his day, he had a penchant for prostitutes. He haunts the roadside, walking and swinging a lantern with unseen hands (that had a habit of strangling unsuspecting hookers).

Meanwhile, the tortured souls of those who have leaped to their deaths haunt the soaring expanse of the Arroyo Seco bridge in Pasadena, California. When the moon is full and conditions are right, the weary Route 66 traveler may very well come across one of these suicidal phantoms seeking peaceful release from this earthly realm. It's all a matter of timing and an open mind.

It's the same story for the dozens of other so-called "hot spots" that occupy the forgotten nooks and crannies of old 66 where motorists have lost their lives. The bridge at Devils Elbow, Missouri, is an active venue for spectral disturbances; the victims who died in

traffic accidents there are often seen clamoring for attention. The same is true for the Bushland "Death Trap," the dangerous underpass and treacherous S curve in Bushland, Texas. During its early years, this site claimed countless lives and was a prime spot for strange spirits; traffic was finally rerouted around it.

But the "Humpback Hauntings" are perhaps the most memorable of Route 66 tall tales. Along a ghostly stretch of the old road between Weatherford and El Reno, Oklahoma, travelers and residents alike have reported sighting a decrepit old man with a humped back, dressed in a fedora and trench coat, slowly making his way along the side of the highway. His dress is appropriate, because it's often on foggy or rainy nights that the apparition makes his ghostly presence known.

As people tell it, the old codger is picked up by any Good Samaritan who might be passing by. He climbs into the car but makes

The recurring theme of the vanishing hitchhiker was visited by Rod Serling himself in the 1950 television series *The Twilight Zone*. "The Hitch-Hiker" first aired on January 22, 1960.

The vanishing hitchhiker never seems to get anywhere. His sole purpose seems to be the bedevilment of those who unwittingly choose to pick him up.

nary a sound, despite repeated interrogation. "Where you going, Mister? What's your name?" There is no response.

After some miles, the driver becomes complacent with the situation, and, of course, that's when the apparition makes his move. Without warning, he reaches for the door handle and attempts to jump from the moving vehicle. Frantic, the driver stops the car to let the man out, but he has already vanished! The driver gets back on the road, but, lo and behold, he comes upon the humpbacked man just a few miles down the road, still walking.

So goes the tale of the vanishing hitchhiker, who actually became the subject of a classic *Twilight Zone* episode in 1960. In this Rod Serling teleplay, Nan Adams is traveling across the country when she encounters a strange hitchhiker. She sees him on numerous occasions during the trip and for some reason can't seem to shake him. She becomes convinced that he's trying to kill her.

Eventually, she tries to run over the man to free herself but in a macabre twist discovers that she is, in fact, dead. Her car flipped over at the start of her journey, and the pesky hitchhiker is merely the grim reaper. Distraught, she returns to the car and looks in the visor's vanity mirror. Instead of her reflection, Nan sees the hitchhiker in her place. "I believe you're going . . . my way?" he inquires.

If you're traveling along one of the old stretches of Route 66 and see an old man hobbling down the side of the roadway, think twice before you stop.

2.
TRI-COUNTY TRUCK STOP GHOSTS

VILLA RIDGE, MISSOURI

The 1940s Diamonds was Streamline efficiency. These were the glory days of this roadside stop, with many of today's ghosts already staking their claim.

Located near the junctions of US Highway 50, Missouri Route 100, and old Route 66 in Villa Ridge, Missouri, it's no wonder that the Tri-County Truck Stop has had more than its share of strange and unexplained paranormal happenings. During its heyday, while operating under the name The Diamonds, it was a jewel in the crown of America's Main Street, serving more than one million customers every year.

With so many souls passing through, there can be little doubt that heartache and tragedy darkened the doors of this establishment more than once, creating the existential ripples in the fabric of space and time that eventually led to a wave of unexplained phenomena.

The story of this place began at the turn of the century, when a young man by the name of Spencer Groff recognized the earning potential of this roadside nexus (he wrote a book about his exploits called *Diamond Dust*). Groff started selling fruit and produce from a small stand and by 1923 had established a popular store at the crossroads, known among locals as the "banana stand."

The business flourished and by 1927 was rebuilt and opened as The Diamonds, a much more extensive operation. Former busboy Louis Eckelkamp took over in 1933 and rebuilt the entire business in the

1960s after a fire burned it to cinders. The reborn establishment was a grand showcase for everything related to travel and the automobile. The building took its styling cues from Streamline Moderne, including a service station, bus ticket depot, curio store, popcorn stand, travel bureau, cafeteria, and full-service restaurant—all under one roof.

The Tri-County Truck Stop was the last iteration of The Diamonds, the place once known as the "Old Reliable Eating Place." Interstate truckers became the new target audience, but apparently the place's unseen "residents" were not pleased with the transition. About that time, strange activity began to manifest itself. A spirit named George suddenly got a little bit too touchy-feely with waitresses. Other visual disturbances were noted. Why were ghosts who had been waiting in the woodwork for so many years making their appearance?

The hauntings intensified, and in September 2006, the Tri-County was closed for "health and safety" reasons. The boarded-up windows and oversized parking lot now devoid of cars made the place look haunted, and soon after, rumors of ghosts and other hauntings intensified. Former employees and visitors began revealing their encounters.

In 2006, the disturbances were officially investigated by a team of modern-day ghostbusters, a group known as the Paranormal Task Force (PTF) based in Saint Louis, Missouri. A team of special investigators from their office attended, and the event was scheduled to take place from 9:30 p.m. to 4:00 a.m.

Indeed, it proved to be a long night for even the seasoned investigators, who witnessed many oddities they could not explain. Investigators recorded a coffee pot that crashed to the floor after sliding across a counter; others revealed that they were "touched" by unseen forces (George, is that you?). In the poltergeist department, doors opened on their own, and there was banging and

The second Diamonds was run by Louis Eckelkamp and his crew. Take note of the faces; who can say that there aren't one or two ghosts in the making?

rattling in the kitchen area when no one was present. A video camera even recorded a blue phosphorescent presence (the video was later posted on YouTube).

The PTF team's final analysis concluded, "It is the opinion of Paranormal Task Force that enough unexplainable evidence was captured and/or experienced to substantiate the high probability of an actual haunting or paranormal activity." Today, the team continues to look for information on a man who used to live in the basement of the establishment between the 1950s and 1970s. He was believed to have some mental impairment and was last seen running into the woods behind the restaurant following an altercation.

Today, many regard the Tri-County Truck Stop as one of the most haunted sites along old Route 66. To satiate the public's curiosity, the PTF often stages tours of this historic roadside attraction. In 2015, participants were invited on a three-hour adventure to learn about the quirky history of the landmark and, in the process, witness whatever ghostly apparitions were to be seen frolicking within its walls—no actors, props, or gimmicks.

From the roadway, the Tri-County Truck Stop appears to be an operation devoid of life. But inside, cloaked by shadows and the cover of darkness, the denizens of the dark side still patronize their favorite diner, a rogue's gallery of strange beings and ghostly creatures clamoring for another cup of coffee and more pie.

OPPOSITE TOP: By the time The Diamonds became the Tri-County Truck Stop, the hauntings had already begun. Generations of visitors had come and gone, some deciding to stay.

OPPOSITE BOTTOM: The way the Tri-County is situated at the convergence of two major roadways plays a part in its paranormal activities; it's the intersection of two powerful energy bands in space and time.

BELOW: Now abandoned, the living portion of the Tri-County has given up all possession to the ghosts of the past, which are free to roam about its now-deserted interior.

3.
HOTEL MONTE VISTA HAUNTING

FLAGSTAFF, ARIZONA

ABOVE: A beautiful building in its own right, the historic Monte Vista Hotel has a unique character. Who wouldn't want to haunt such comfortable surroundings?

OPPOSITE: Time lapse light streamers remind us of the paranormal activities that have been reported inside this structure, with many unexplained sightings and ghosts.

During the 1920s, citizens of Flagstaff, Arizona, were eager to improve the local amenities for town visitors. At the time, overnight accommodations were pretty spartan, and the city had little to offer people in the way of creature comforts. Community leaders began to brainstorm. "Why not build a comfortable, upscale hotel for tourists and visitors?"

In the spring of 1926, prominent local leaders kicked off a fundraiser to gather the money needed to build the new tourist magnet. One of the more well-off donors was novelist Zane Grey, a prolific writer who had written *Riders of the Purple Sage* and whose novels were made into more than one hundred motion pictures. In just a few months, the effort raised $200,000, enough to build the dream.

On New Year's Day 1927, one year after Route 66 was born, the seventy-three-room Community Hotel officially opened its doors.

Apparitions have been spotted at the Monte Vista in all areas, including the lobby. Sometimes visitors check in but never completely check out.

The structure housed the local post office and offices of the *Coconino Sun* newspaper. Locals and visitors alike were impressed by the luxurious accommodations, but the name fell flat. Soon after, a contest was held to find a new one. A twelve-year-old submitted the winning name, Monte Vista, which in Spanish means "mountain view."

In the coming years, the hotel became a favorite layover for vacationers traveling Route 66. Movie producers and actors made it their home when filming westerns in the area. Mary Costigan (the second woman in the world to obtain a radio broadcast license, call letters KFXY) moved her station into the hotel facilities in 1927. Later, the hotel installed the state's first self-service Otis elevator. During Prohibition, with bootlegging in full swing, an onsite bar called the Cocktail Lounge wet people's whistle. A light high atop the structure served as a local emergency beacon in the 1930s.

Oddly enough, a clandestine network of underground tunnels ran from the University of Flagstaff to the downtown area, with easy access available to the Monte Vista. In some of the roomier tunnel alcoves, explorers who plumbed the less savory depths of Flagstaff uncovered all manner of vice, including dens used to smoke opium, equipment designed to make moonshine, and machines that facilitated illegal gambling.

Today, many of these quirky earthly facts about the hotel have been forgotten, replaced by lurid tales of paranormal activities and resident ghosts. There's good reason; more than once, visitors have seen barstools and drinks move around on their own, a phantom boy who runs through the hallways, and a transparent couple who likes to trip the light fantastic.

After hearing the faint sounds of an infant crying in the basement or seeing a lightbulb unscrew itself, even the skeptical admit that they too feel the hair on the back of their neck stand up. At the Hotel Monte Vista, the feeling that someone is watching you is all too familiar.

One of the more famous ghosts that haunts the halls of the Monte Vista is the "phantom bellboy." Dressed in the costume of another age, the boy and his red coat are well remembered. Even famous western actor John Wayne powwowed with the service-oriented apparition during his 1940s stay. When quizzed about the poltergeist, the Duke reported that he "seemed nice and not threatening at all." Whatever his intentions, the spirit routinely knocks on people's doors and announces room service, only to vanish when someone answers the door.

Indeed, the Monte Vista has been called the most haunted place in Arizona. But is it really haunted? A few years ago, the television series *Unsolved Mysteries* tried to answer the question when they investigated the story of the Rocking Chair Lady. Apparently, she likes to haunt room 305, and numerous people have reported seeing her in the window, rocking back and forth. Guests have seen the chair move on its own too—and heard knocking sounds emanating from within the vacant room.

Still not convinced? Take a break from your Route 66 trip to spend the night there. The best evidence is the kind that's seen with your own two eyes—or is it? For if ghosts truly do haunt the halls of the Hotel Monte Vista, you need only open your mind to see them. Have a nice stay . . .

A trick of the light or just fogged film created by an anomaly in the darkroom? The Monte Vista may surprise you with its paranormal manifestations.

4.
AMERICA'S LAST LIVING GHOST TOWN

OATMAN, ARIZONA

Back in the day, Oatman, Arizona, was a remote mining town built on the discovery of gold. Today, it's a tourist attraction worth stopping for on the way out West.

Ghost towns are curious things. They exist as giant question marks, beckoning us for answers: How can a town be abandoned lock, stock, and barrel and left to decay without a thought? Where did all the residents go and what catastrophe caused them to vacate their lives? In a land so prosperous, is it possible for a whole town to lose its livelihood?

Zoom in on the Arizona stretch of old Route 66, and you may very well find the answers. Located near the border of Nevada on the Colorado River, the village of Oatman exists as a prime example of a place that refuses to give up the ghost, as it were. Here is a site that managed to defy the economic cycles of boom and bust, the loss of tourism, and the onslaught of time. In spite of everything that has tried to kill it off, it continues to exist. Some call it America's last living ghost town.

Once upon a time, Oatman was the busiest outpost in this part of the Black Mountains. In fact, it was one of the most famous gold-producing towns in the West. After two lucky miners struck it rich with a $10 million find in 1915, news spread fast. Individual prospectors and mining concerns took note, and for the next two years, there was real gold rush underway. Oatman rose to become the pinnacle of mining in the region and produced the lion's share of gold during the years between 1902 and 1940.

The mining settlement that eventually became a town started making a legend for itself as far back as 1851, when a young Illinois girl by the name of Olive Oatman made the arduous trek West with her family but upon her arrival was abducted by Apache warriors and forced into slavery. They traded her to the Mohaves, and her face was tattooed in the style of the tribe. Five years later, she gained her freedom at Fort Yuma, Arizona.

In 1863, legendary mountain man and prospector Johnny Moss staked several claims in the Black Mountains and named one of them "Moss" after himself. A second claim, called the "Oatman," took its name from the Illinois girl who met her unlucky fate so many years ago. The abduction story had legs, and by 1909, it was so ingrained into local lore that the town officially changed its name to Oatman in honor of the young girl.

Oatman mining increased during the mid-1910s when the United Eastern Mining Company moved in after the success of the Tom Reed

The sights along Main Street in Oatman, Arizona, are exactly what you would expect to see in a place billed as "America's Last Living Ghost Town."

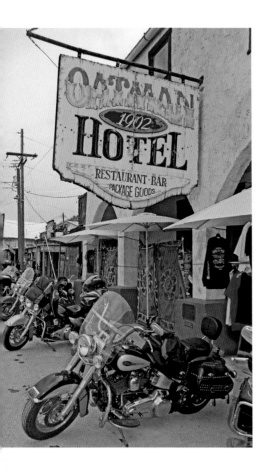

ABOVE: The Oatman Hotel began as a tent city and was called the Drulin in 1902. Of course, it's completely haunted, with the friendly poltergeist "Oatie" leading the cast of apparitions.

ABOVE RIGHT: Over the mountain passes on the way to Oatman, the Arizona scenery is a stark reminder of how dangerous it once was to travel across the country.

gold mine. However, the boom was not without tragedy. In 1921, a raging fire burned down most of Oatman's buildings. By some small miracle, the Oatman Hotel (built in 1902) was spared from the inferno. Today, it remains as the oldest two-story adobe structure in Arizona's Mohave County, officially registered as a historical landmark.

These days, the Oatman Hotel sets the stage for most of the paranormal activities in town. The proprietors like to play up the idea of a friendly poltergeist known as Oatie, reportedly the ghost of one William Ray Flour. A miner of Irish descent, Flour supposedly drank too much booze and died behind the hotel. At the time, his compatriots overlooked his body for two days before hastily burying it in a shallow grave.

In 1924, the major mines shut down, and residents turned to Route 66 as their savior. Oatman is located between Kingman and Needles, and motorists had no choice but to pass through town on Highway 66 (Oatman Road). Unfortunately, the switchbacks of the Sitgreaves Pass were notoriously dangerous. A more direct local route between the two towns was planned, and by the time it was finished in 1952, people had already written Oatman's obituary.

The ghosts began taking over during the 1960s, when most of the living population vacated. Tourism, mining, and other modes of income were nonexistent for most of the 1970s and 1980s. Many of

Today, Oatman is overrun by wild mules, part of the tourist attraction that is downtown. The town began as a mining camp after prospectors struck a $10 million gold find in 1915.

the buildings went into disrepair, and wild burros began to move in as human residents moved out. Oddly enough, the burros are still among the most popular tourist attractions in Oatman and can often be seen wandering the empty streets.

With the resurgence of gold, mining activity comes and goes these days in Oatman. Nostalgia has become the big appeal, with daily reenactments of gunfights and all the other accouterments of the Old West put on display. In a somewhat strange turn of events, curious people have become the modern-day ghosts that haunt this town. Here today and gone tomorrow, they leave behind only their tourist dollars and trash as physical evidence that they were ever here.

5.
THE MIRACULOUS WEEPING ICON

CICERO, ILLINOIS

The weeping icon of Mary, "Our Lady of Cicero," has drawn huge crowds to Saint Nicholas since it began to emit moisture in December 1986.

When an ordinary object exhibits supernatural tendencies—that is, it moves, bleeds, or weeps—it is no doubt a portent of evil and something to recoil from in fear. However, when a religious statue, painting, or artifact is seen doing something characterized as "human," the faithful fall to their knees in sheer reverence. It's almost as if something heavenly or protective has revealed its presence, reassuring us that everything will be all right.

That's precisely the kind of encouragement a strange and unexplained mystery of a biblical nature gave to the members of the Saint George Antiochian Orthodox Church, a house of worship located in Cicero, Illinois. On April 22, 1994, parishioners rejoiced and praised God after they witnessed a modern-day miracle seemingly tailor-made for them.

The congregation had gathered in the assembly hall of Saint George, engaged in traditional Lenten chanting. (During Lent, the believer repents their sins, does penance, and denies themselves certain things, replicating the sacrifice of Jesus Christ's forty-day desert journey.) Archpriest Nicholas Dahdal was preparing for the Friday evening services and hosting a guest, Father Douglas Wyper.

In what seemed a simultaneous instant, Wyper, Dahdal, and the congregation noticed something odd on the surface of the Theotokos— the icon of the Virgin Mary and the Baby Jesus mounted on the church's iconostasis. Streaks were coming from the eyes of the holy mother! The strange phenomena continued into the evening, and at the stroke of midnight, witnesses confirmed that four distinct trails of tears flowed to the bottom of the icon.

In the days that followed, the decision was made to have the icon examined. Before word of the miracle spread too far, Dahdal wanted to be 100 percent sure that the tears were genuine. Elsewhere,

charlatans hoping to fool the faithful have created tears with smeared animal fat, which slowly liquefies at room temperature. Calcium chloride is also a favorite because it pulls moisture from the air and creates a similar effect. But Wesson oil is the favorite: fraudsters strategically splash droplets for maximum impact.

To investigate the phenomena, the church brought in his eminence Metropolitan Philip, who was at the time the primate of the Antiochian Orthodox Christian Archdiocese of North America. Upon seeing the weeping religious icon, he made the statement, "I therefore

Pictured is the Saint George Antiochian Orthodox Church in Cicero, Illinois. In the Eastern Orthodox tradition, the iconostasis is a wall between the church body and the sanctuary that is filled with icons.

designate this Icon of the Theotokos at St. George Antiochian Orthodox Church as 'The Miraculous Lady of Cicero, Illinois,' and encourage our faithful everywhere to seek her intercessions." Archpriest Dahdal concurred with the finding, reminding the Doubting Thomases that the icon was behind locked doors twenty-four hours a day and scrutinized quite closely.

Today, the icon receives many more visitors than just faithful locals. More than one million pilgrims from all parts of the globe have found their way to the Theotokos at Saint George to witness what they perceive as a miracle.

While it is an obvious draw for religious Americans from all sects of Christianity, it's curious to note that a good many nonreligious people have experienced miracles in the presence of the famed Theotokos. Under the purveyance of the icon, the church reports that the sick are healed and the lame made to walk again. Since the divine tears first began to flow, many miraculous acts have occurred at the church.

To this day, the icon still weeps, and the church continues to reap the benefits of her miraculous tears. They have made it their mission to spread the healing powers of the icon far and wide. To date, church personnel have collected and sent the teardrops to more than one thousand religious organizations around the world (tiny bottles of oil mixed with the tears). In the two months following the appearance of the first tears, Saint George sent out more than one hundred thousand cotton swabs imbued with the miraculous tears. "We feel very blessed here, especially because we have been able to accommodate all these people," Dahdal said.

With the US Mail, the miraculous powers of the weeping icon have spilled out onto the roadways. On March 29, 2015, the street across from the church received the honorary name of Our Lady of Cicero Court. Now, the real miracle is that the icon is connected to the maze of surface streets linked up with Route 66 and the countless souls who traverse her miles.

OPPOSITE: Behold the miracle, ye of little faith: eight orthodox bishops have examined the weeping icon phenomena and have declared that the tears are genuine.

6.
SPOOK LIGHT ON DEVIL'S PROMENADE

QUAPAW, OKLAHOMA

Fig. 6. Terreur de paysans de Salagnac (Corrèze) en voyant passer un éclair en boule.

Many explanations have been handed out to explain the mysterious lights, including that it's a ball lightning, a rare but documented natural phenomenon.

In every state cut asunder by Route 66, one is sure to encounter ghosts and other unexplained phenomena. But in Oklahoma there exists one unsolved mystery that is as difficult to forget as it is to explain—once you see it for yourself. It's a phenomenon regularly witnessed along the place called Devil's Promenade, a well-known site just a stone's throw from the old road in Quapaw, Oklahoma. The locals call it "Spook Light."

Will-o'-the-wisps are common phenomena in both American and global folk tales. Said to be "fairy lights" or "omen lights," they are often reported to lead people into dangerous or deadly situations. Usually, there's an element of revenge underlying these stories. Spook lights, as storytellers refer to them in domestic folklore, definitely have this aspect behind them.

Often related to deep-seated tensions that arose between early European visitors and American Indians, they are a way of remembering history and also a warning against future transgressions of the same kind. There's something eerie about the idea of a glowing orb with a personality of its own, and that could be why the spook light haunts American folklore.

On occasion, the bobbing lights have also been seen in nearby states, leading some to refer to them as the "Tri-State Spook Lights." Witnesses describe the lights near the Devil's Promenade as the

size of a basketball, and even though many tales confirm their visual manifestation, they are still a rare event. "Spook Road," the path officially designated E50, is the most likely place to find them.

Multiple agencies and scientific concerns have studied the phenomena, including the US Army Corps of Engineers. To date, nothing has adequately explained the strange lights. Local folklore has stepped in to fill the gap, attempting in its own way to explain the meaning of the ghostly lights and to ease the minds of those who have witnessed them.

One of the more popular explanations for the Spook Light is a paranormal one. Oklahoma was the point of terminus for the Trail of

Although the spook light orbs are less defined in their overall appearance, this fanciful depiction evokes the mystery of the unexplained woodlands phenomenon.

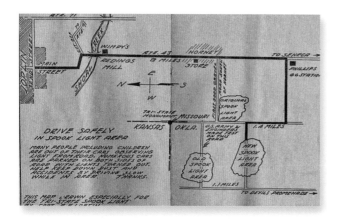

Tears, the forced exodus of American Indians from their homelands in the southeast United States during the 1870s. It's easy to see how the haunting light might be the ghost of an American Indian, a spirit angered by the fact that it was forced from its ancestral home to a strange land.

Another tale tells of a Quapaw woman who fell in love with a Quapaw man. The two eloped when her father refused to let the poor suitor and his daughter marry because the suitor was unable to pay the dowry. A search party pursued them, and, facing capture, they made a suicide pact and jumped in the nearby river. Their ghosts became today's spook lights.

But this fable is just the beginning. Others say that the spook light is the ghost of a miner searching for his missing family. Another gruesome yarn spins the tale of a decapitated Osage chief searching for his head by the light of a lantern. There is even a small fringe of believers who think that the lights are the result of extraterrestrials.

Others believe that the lights have a logical explanation. Over the years, one top explanation involves the headlights of cars in the distance. But no roads come from opposing directions, and there is no practical way any vehicle could drive through the hilly woods.

Even finding the Devil's Promenade, a local name for the road, can prove tricky. To see the strange lights for yourself, take Exit 4 off Interstate 44. Then follow Highway 86 south for about six miles until you arrive at the junction with Route BB. Follow this road until it ends, and then take another right. In one mile, you will come upon E50. Congratulations, you made it to the Devil's Promenade!

Locals say that the best place to see the lights is about one and a half miles down the road. Not only is this site the darkest, but it's also the one with the most reported supernatural activity. Here you will be able to ponder the mystery yourself and come to your own conclusions. Is the spook light the lantern light of an Osage chief, the lamplight of a worried miner, or the ghosts of lovers waltzing through the Ozark's dark trees? If you stick around long enough, maybe you will find out.

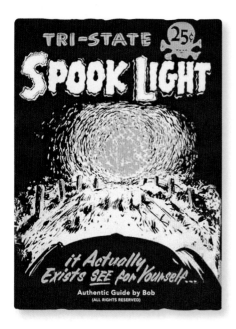

TOP: The best place to see the spook light has moved over the years. It's still out there waiting for all those who are ready to witness a little bit of magic and wonder.

ABOVE: *Tri-State Spook Light* (by Bob) was published during the 1960s to aid Route 66 travelers who were wishing to find and witness these amazing orbs for themselves.

OPPOSITE: Many have said that the spook light is the result of car headlamps, but the way the roads are situated in the various viewing spots, the theory simply does not line up.

TOP FIVE

WEIRD to go and WEIRD to do

1 2 3 4 5

BRAUM'S MILK BOTTLE

Route 66, Oklahoma City, Oklahoma

Since it was built in 1930, this isolated curiosity—hemmed in on all sides by roads—has advertised milk products. Over the decades, it has seen activity in a number of iterations, including a dry cleaner, realty office, fruit market, Vietnamese grocery, and barbecue shack.

SHOE TREE

Old Route 66, Amboy, California

Although this shoe tree has since collapsed from the weight of all the shoes, there is still a small scattering of similar sites along 66. In the inner city, a pair of sneakers suspended on a wire represents a fallen comrade. In the outskirts, it signifies a transition to a new life.

GROOM CROSS

Interstate 40, Groom, Texas

"The Cross of Our Lord Jesus Christ" shoots up nineteen stories from the Texas panhandle, 2.5 million pounds of steel bankrolled by yet another Texas millionaire. You'll see it for miles as you approach, but be sure to stop and witness for yourself the reproduction of Jesus's tomb.

KOREAN WAR MEMORIAL

Route 66, Oatman, Arizona

High on the ridge cliffs just off of mile marker 21 near Oatman, look for an American flag blowing in the breeze. It's part of a handbuilt stone monument honoring veterans of the Korean War. It was built by eighty-year-old vet Charles "Uncle Charlie" Hicks for his brother-in-law Joe Van Landingham.

ALBUQUERQUE MURAL

Central Avenue, Albuquerque, New Mexico

One of many Route 66 murals worth taking the time to check out and see in person, this Jesus-themed example is done in a comic book and graffiti style. It takes up the otherwise blank space on a commercial building on Central Avenue (Route 66) in Albuquerque, New Mexico.

MEMORABLE STRUCTURES AND CRAZY CONSTRUCTS

Memorable Structures and Crazy Constructs is a showcase of the far-out buildings, signs, and structures that infuse Route 66 with a unique personality and charm. Whether it's a mimetic structure seeking to invoke whimsy or a construct of exaggerated modern architecture, these are the buildings that take the leap from the ordinary to the extraordinary, modern-day monuments that compel us to pull over and grab our camera phones.

1.
EAT AND SLEEP IN A WIGWAM

HOLBROOK, ARIZONA

The Wigwam Motel in Holbrook, Arizona, was number six in the series of motels. Chester Lewis built the chain based on architect Frank Redford's clever Cave City, Kentucky, "wigwam" designs.

As a child, Frank Redford traveled with his parents extensively. On one trip to Long Beach, California, he couldn't believe his eyes when he saw a snack stand shaped like an ice cream cone. Later, on a trip to South Dakota, he saw his first wigwam.

Over the years, the two ideas blended. Inspired by the geometric similarity of the two structures, he wondered why one couldn't house a roadside business—such as a restaurant and filling station—in a structure that looked like a teepee.

By the time he turned thirty, Redford had picked a spot in Horse Cave, Kentucky, and began building a lunchroom and service station to match the colorful picture he had painted in his imagination. By 1933, his roadside attraction was finished, and unsuspecting tourists who visited Mammoth Cave bore witness to the fantastic: giant teepees along Highway 31E!

For the time, long before Disneyland and other extravagant theme parks, his roadside attraction was a big deal. No one had ever seen a service station office housed in a sixty-foot-high wigwam accompanied by two smaller teepees that served as restrooms.

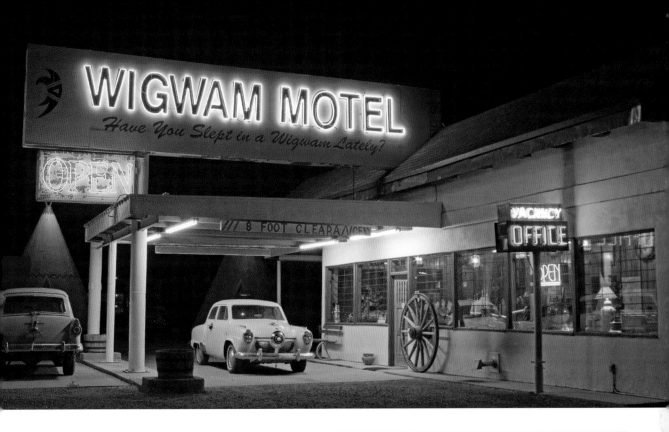

The front facade of Wigwam Village Motel #6 is a total time warp for Route 66 tourists visiting Holbrook, Arizona, complete with colorful neon lighting and resident classic cars.

Despite pushing American Indian stereotypes to the extreme, with little, if any, sensitivity for indigenous cultures, Redford's idea brought in plenty of customers. Ironically, only a few decades earlier, similar folks moving west by wagon train were obsessed with eliminating American Indians. During a January 1886 speech in New York, none other than President Teddy Roosevelt said, "I don't go so far as to think that the only good Indians are dead Indians, but I believe nine out of every ten are."

In these modern times, the idea of a wigwam motel might be viewed as pure kitsch and a little bit tacky, but along vintage Route 66, the concept fits in without a hitch.

Redford's teepee cottages provided a grand illusion but were nothing like the real thing (which employed the extensive use of animal hides). The primary framing was engineered to be as sturdy as a stick-built suburban rambler, despite the cone-shaped arrangement. Four metal poles poked through at the apex of the cone to provide the effect of real lodge poles. On the outside, the skeleton was covered with commercially made tarpaper and a layer of stucco.

Redford painted the teepees white and accented them with red zigzag edging on the top. More rickrack circled below, leading the eye to a diamond-shaped window. Builders hung standard doors in an egress and sculpted the 3D surround out of concrete mortar made to look like a rolled-back flap of hide.

The strange (and whitewashed) truth about the wigwams is that, in their original form, they featured a swastika symbol directly above the front door! The sacred religious symbol was known to the Navajo tribe as one of good luck. After Adolf Hitler and his Third Reich adopted the icon, its use was, of course, stigmatized. Revisionists removed all vestiges of the swastika, including those that adorned the Wigwam Villages.

Of course, sleeping in an authentic American Indian teepee wouldn't provide the level of comfort most twentieth century travelers were used to. But in the world of roadside America, the teepee was re-imagined for comfort with insulated walls, knotty pine paneling,

"Eat and Sleep in a Wigwam" may seem like just another catch phrase, but when you see these units illuminated at dusk, they exude a certain welcoming charm that pulls you in.

and decorative molding. Ceramic tiles covered the floors and walls of the indoor bathrooms. Overnight guests had all the comforts of home, including a sink and shower with hot and cold running water and a flush toilet. Whereas early natives relied on fire for warmth, the steam-powered radiators here provided heat.

Specially selected furnishings further played on stereotypes of the Wild West. Redford had beds, chairs, and night tables custom crafted from rough hickory (with the real bark still in place). Of course, this gave the lodger a sense that they were roughing it. To keep the authenticity going, the rooms had real Apache blankets and Navajo rugs.

After Duncan Hines heard about the operation, he wrote up a review in his book *Lodging for a Night*, a sort of Yelp! for the age. Redford soon had investors eager to franchise, and in 1937, he built a second location on Highway 31W. Five more villages followed, starting in New Orleans, Orlando, and Birmingham. Route 66 gained its very first location (number six) in the town of Holbrook, Arizona, and in 1947, the Foothill Boulevard stretch of 66 hosted the seventh and last Wigwam Village in the city of San Bernardino, California.

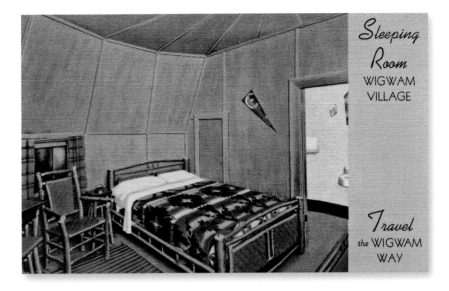

TOP: The wigwam interiors were originally outfitted with rustic wood furniture and came complete with bathrooms that featured hot and cold running water.

ABOVE: In Cave City, Kentucky, Wigwam Village #2 was admired by many who stopped by to spend the night. The execution of the idea was spot on, despite it being a caricature of American Indian life.

2.
AN HOMAGE TO THE CADILLAC

AMARILLO, TEXAS

Interstate 40 took over the job of transporting motorists out west when Route 66 was decommissioned. But old road or new, it still takes days to traverse the Lone Star State.

If you were to construct a monument in honor of the automobile and the braggadocio of American car culture, what sort of vehicle would you propose? Perhaps you might suggest the Ford Model T. With its everyman's utility and reliability, it would be a good choice. Unfortunately, there would be little to work with regarding sex appeal and overall pizazz. A design that takes its cues from a horse-drawn carriage is mundane at best.

More appropriate would be an automobile that represented a certain level of luxury, an over-the-top marque that, down through the ages, has exuded the image of success. It would have to be a car that combined the unashamed sexiness of Marilyn Monroe with the adrenaline-pumping energy of a modern jet fighter. Of course, that car would have to be made in the United States by the muscle of American workers, the chrome and lacquer offspring of the Motor City itself. And when it comes to Detroit iron, what car is more iconic than the Cadillac?

Indeed, the Ant Farm—the San Francisco art collective behind the Cadillac Ranch in Amarillo, Texas—could not have chosen a more beautiful car when they came up with the idea for their famous roadside car sculpture back in 1974. At the time, artists Chip Lord, Hudson Marquez, and Doug Michels had concocted a crazy idea for an installation made of full-size automobiles—planted in the ground, of course.

Like many artists, they were not in a position to fund the unorthodox artwork themselves. Enter local art patron and millionaire

Stanley Marsh 3 (he thought that Roman numerals were pretentious). The Ant Farm approached him with their idea to build a public monument to Cadillacs, and he promised an answer to their proposed funding plan by April Fool's Day.

He was true to his word, but Marsh had a few ideas of his own. First, he asked the group to come up with something that would inspire "delight and bewilderment" among the people of Amarillo. He happened to be a prankster known for his odd showcases, particularly a place called the Dynamite Museum in Amarillo. At one point, his sense of humor earned him a place of prominence on President Richard Nixon's "enemies list." Apparently, writing to Pat Nixon about including one of her hats in a museum dedicated to decadent art was a bad idea!

After Marsh agreed, the iconic Route 66 landmark was born, right there off the highway in the middle of a wheat field. The sculpture showcased the birth and death of various Cadillac features, the most notable being the tailfin (which spanned from 1949 to 1962). The ten cars were planted in the ground nose first and set at an angle to copy the Great Pyramid of Giza in Egypt.

Created by the Ant Farm Group for Stanley Marsh 3, Amarillo's Cadillac Ranch endures as a tribute to Detroit iron and the cars that helped make America great.

Unfortunately, the sculpture wasn't that well received by the local community when it debuted. At the time, Texans who had any appreciation for modern installation art were few and far between. Some critics suggested that the sculpture was hardly an original piece and more like a derivative assemblage of parts. After all, famous automotive designers, such as Harley Earl, who designed the Cadillac, deserved the credit for the sleek lines, angular forms, and soaring tailfins. The only "art" involved in the Amarillo installation was planting them in the ground.

Art critics aside, the Cadillac installation soon began a never-ending cycle of visual transformation. The cars started out in their original factory colors, but that didn't last long. Soon, the entire assemblage was whitewashed for a television commercial. At one time, Marsh had the Caddies covered in pink to honor the birthday of his wife, Wendy! Then, when Ant Farm artist Doug Michels died, the installation turned a flat black in mourning. In 2012, all the colors of the rainbow commemorated Gay Pride Day.

Strangely enough, graffiti became an integral part of Cadillac Ranch. One might even suggest that it has superseded the importance of the original installation itself.

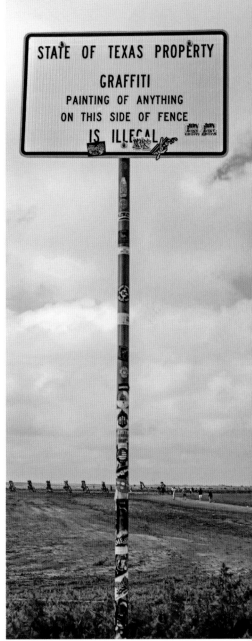

ABOVE: When traveling through Amarillo, Texas, on the great American road trip, make sure that you're stocked up with plenty of spray paint, especially if you plan to contribute to the art.

OPPOSITE: Layered with heavy globs of paint, it's fair to say that within twenty more years the Cadillac Ranch could very well be nothing more than mounds of congealed paint.

Although painting the Cadillac cars is supposedly illegal, the paint is so thick on some of the metal surfaces that the underlying structure is quickly disappearing.

3.
ARCADIA'S ROUND RED BARN

ARCADIA, OKLAHOMA

During the 1890s, standard barn construction in America was classified by three distinct styles of architecture: the Dutch barn, the Pennsylvania barn, and the English barn. While each one featured its own particular nuances in terms of architectural styling, they all had one common denominator—they were based on a cuboid shape that had four perpendicular sides.

Though rectilinear barns were predominant throughout the eighteenth century, it was the religious sect known as the Shakers who built the first truly round barn in 1826, using stones for the walls. Their communal lifestyle made easy work of large construction projects, particularly when it came to hauling, shaping, and stacking heavy stones.

In the years that followed, builders discovered that clay tiles were the perfect medium for constructing circular structures, especially if you had a minimal amount of manpower. With the total diameter of the structure calculated ahead of time, architects could predict the exact size and curvature of each tile block. Craftsman cast the individual tiles and then—like pieces in a Lego set—stacked them to form a curved, circular enclosure.

ABOVE: Arcadia's Round Barn was created using specialized building techniques, most notably the use of jigs and the wet-bending of wood to form the curved superstructure.

OPPOSITE: Before its restoration, Arcadia's Round Barn was in danger of collapsing. Fortunately, local community efforts stepped in and saved another roadside gem for future posterity.

The interior acoustics of the Round Barn make it perfectly suited for concerts and other musical performances, something this structure has seen much of over the decades.

Enter William Odor, the mastermind of Round Barn of Arcadia, Oklahoma. He was of sound mind and body but wanted to build a round barn, not of stone but entirely out of wood. He would stop at nothing until his dream became a reality. And so, in 1898, he used good old American stick-to-it-iveness and hard work to git 'er done, developing homegrown methods of construction along the way.

Fortunately, his wife, Myrna, was the understanding type who backed her husband. While the naysayers cried that it would be impossible to build by himself, she laughed to herself as William found a way. Native burr oak was plentiful, so he decided to harvest nearby trees for lumber. But this was just the beginning of the process—since saws only cut logs straight.

With no formal engineering training, Odor found a way to bend the boards into the curved pieces he needed. First, he borrowed boatbuilding techniques and soaked the wood in water. Once the parts were sufficiently waterlogged, he forced them into a special jig that he made, transforming straight boards into segments of a predetermined radius. Once they had the right shape, he applied them to the frame.

Upon completion, everyone could see that Odor's two-story barn was without a doubt a thing of beauty. It seemed a shame to use something so attractive to house nothing but hay and farm animals. Soon, locals began hanging out at the barn, and the second story became a community venue for local dances. Inside, the roof had a cathedral-like quality and acoustics perfect for musical performances.

When Route 66 came a-callin', it rolled straight through the town, bringing a fresh supply of admirers. There was simply no way the people speeding past in their automobiles could ignore the big, round red barn. The circular wonder became one of the most popular venues on Oklahoma 66 at which to record a Kodak moment.

The Oklahoma stretch of Route 66 meanders through many small towns, offering a glimpse of what it was once like to travel cross country without interstates.

As years rolled by, ownership of the barn changed numerous times. With each successive owner, the zeal for the original concept diminished. Round buildings were no longer a big deal. By the time Route 66 was at the end of its glory days, the barn had begun to deteriorate.

Tragedy struck in 1988 when the roof caved in, and estimates indicated that it would cost a minimum of $165,000 to repair. Fortunately, a retired contractor took interest and sparked a mission to save the barn. He assembled a group of volunteers known as "the Over the Hill Gang," a local crew who solicited donations and sold bricks inscribed with each donor's name. They raised $65,000, enough to cover the restoration if they provided the labor themselves. In 1992, they won the National Preservation Honor Award for their efforts.

Today, Arcadia's big red barn still stands tall. The roomy second floor is still available for weddings, dances, and other special occasions and can host 150 people. There's even a bluegrass concert held every second Sunday of the month from noon until dinner. Best of all, the barn's open to Route 66 visitors seven days a week.

4.
HOLE IN THE WALL CONOCO STATION

COMMERCE, OKLAHOMA

Over the years, Route 66 has been a fertile breeding ground for mile after mile of interesting architecture, especially when it comes to businesses that service cars. During the heyday of America's Main Street, it wasn't unusual for tourists to come across a gas station shaped like an iceberg or one with an office inside a giant teepee.

Unfortunately, most really cool examples of mimetic roadside architecture from motoring's golden age have been razed—that is, if you don't count the "Hole in the Wall" station in Commerce, Oklahoma. The quaint structure endures as a prime example of early service station "house" architecture, the style that Phillips Petroleum made famous with its early designs (this location started as a Phillips 66–branded station).

The strange thing about this service station is its out-of-scale appearance. At first glance, something doesn't seem quite right; one might easily imagine that the station attendants were Lilliputians or even Oompa Loompas—a couple dozen of them pouring out of the office door to welcome the arrival of a new car. The fact is, it's an optical illusion. The narrow depth of the structure makes it look smaller than it is, leading some to believe that it's nothing more than a movie prop or cardboard cutout.

While the intentions behind the quirky construction are a mystery, 66 historians report that the Hole in the Wall was the creation of F. D.

Mitchell, who built the crazy construct in 1931. As the story goes, at one time there was an apartment at one end of the brick wall. It burned down or was destroyed in some sort of accident. Mitchell used the rubble that remained as building materials for the tiny station house. (You can still see a pile of brick behind the main building.) The brick wall became a backdrop for the installation, and now it pops from the roadside like a colorful museum diorama.

The strange little station sat dormant for almost two decades. In 2008, Bobby and Linda Allen came across it, fell in love with the place, and bought it. They wanted to do their part to preserve it for future generations. "So many places are disappearing on Route 66," Linda told reporters. The couple spent the next nine months bringing the "station" back to life.

Today, the operation flies under the vibrant green and red colors of the Conoco brand (founded in 1875 as the Continental Oil and Transportation Company). While the hand-painted sign above the

ABOVE: At Allen's Fillin' Station, everyone is welcome (note the "We Fix Flying Saucers" sign). There's really no gas sold here, just tourist trinkets when the store happens to be open.

OPPOSITE: Gasoline pumps like this 1930s Bowser model used to be topped off with internally illuminated globes that advertised different brands of gasoline with colorful graphics.

Greetings from COMMERCE, OKLA.

TOP: Based in Ogden, Utah, the Continental Oil and Transportation Company was founded in 1875 and was later gobbled up by the Standard Oil Company conglomerate.

ABOVE: Commerce, Oklahoma, could very well be called a one-horse town, but in times past, it was a busy community based on lead and zinc mining. Today, it's another quiet Route 66 town.

door reads "Allen's Fillin' Station," gasoline isn't sold there. As a matter of fact, some nearby business owners that say gasoline was *never* sold here.

When they find it open (during daylight hours on Saturday and after church lets out on Sunday), roadtrippers who traverse this quiet stretch of Oklahoma 66 eagerly stop in to stock up on knickknacks. A must-see side trip is the classic Dairy King located right across the street, where you can get everything from a banana split to a Route 66 cookie shaped like a shield.

During times when the curio shop is closed, people who stop in are more than happy just to take photographs. Pulling your car up to the pump and acting like you are filling it up with one of the hoses is a favorite setup.

Located almost in the middle of nowhere, the Hole in the Wall Conoco Station is a great jumping-off point for those who wish to explore local Oklahoma history. It's interesting to note that the station is located only half a mile from a Bonnie and Clyde historical landmark, which provides fodder for some pretty lurid tales. There, the Barrow Gang gunned down William "Cal" Campbell, a constable and the father of eight children. Campbell was the gang's last victim.

Rumor has it Bonnie and Clyde stopped at the Hole in the Wall for a quick "wipe the windows and check the oil" on their way out of town, but that may be a tall tale. The strange facts are that Bonnie Parker, Clyde Barrow, and Henry Methvin kidnapped Commerce police chief Percy Boyd, drove him into Kansas, and sent him on his way with a clean shirt, a few dollars, and a request from Parker to inform the public that she didn't smoke cigars.

The Hole in the Wall Conoco Station isn't the only claim to fame for Commerce, Oklahoma. Mickey Mantle was born here, earning the nickname "the Commerce Comet" and a statue in his hometown.

5.
THE GLASS HOUSE McDONALD'S

VINITA, OKLAHOMA

This 1977 view of the Azusa, California, shows a Route 66 McDonald's, complete with golden arch building design and "Speedee" mascot on a very low (no doubt due to zoning restrictions) sign.

The McDonald brothers realized their dream when they built their first golden arch–adorned restaurant in Des Plaines, Illinois. Richard McDonald came up with the idea and sketched out on a napkin a small building with an angled roof flanked by two half circles. Architect Stanley Meston humored the brothers, and the golden arches were born.

Today, those arches are synonymous with fast food around the globe. You may not be a fan of the genre, but you have to give props to the story behind the golden *M*—it represents the ability of anyone and everyone to realize the American dream.

So, it comes as no surprise that these golden arches of opportunity are found at numerous spots along Route 66, the highway of promise. The most prominent example is in the town of Vinita, Oklahoma. Here, situated between the turnpike toll plaza and the exit for Vinita, you'll find Phillips 66 gasoline stations and the Glass House McDonald's.

Also known as the Vinita Service Plaza, this site is unlike any ordinary McDonald's. Where a typical eatery would be built upon a foundation situated on a piece of land, this building floats above the Will Rogers Turnpike. Essentially, the building is an arch-style bridge. Its two most prominent features are the arches themselves: massive supports that span the entire width of the highway.

Measuring in at 29,135 square feet, the plaza was the first structure of its kind and, for a while, the largest building in the world that housed a McDonald's. The structure was built back in 1957 when the Will Rogers Turnpike first opened. It's interesting to note that the arches were merely a part of the design and not intended to represent any brand.

At the time, it was one of the flagship locations in the larger chain of Glass House Restaurants, an enterprise operated by the Interstate Host Company out of Los Angeles. During its early years, the Glass House fed travelers in a cafeteria-style restaurant, offering coffee shop comfort food and sumptuous desserts. People traveling the turnpike loved it, but changing tastes and competition led to its demise.

When the Glass House quit the business, the restaurant portion of the site was taken over by Howard Johnson's. Once a burgeoning chain of eateries that spanned the United States and was known for its twenty-eight flavors of ice-cream, "HoJo's" was *the* coffee shop eatery of its day. While the hotel portion of the business survived, the restaurant segment slowly faded from the public eye around

The building that houses the McDonald's restaurant was originally constructed in 1957. When the turnpike first opened, the now-defunct Interstate Host Company ran the show.

ABOVE: The Vinita Service Plaza is the jewel of the Will Rogers Turnpike, complete with two Phillips 66 gas stations and a statue of Will Rogers himself (protected inside the building).

ABOVE RIGHT: With 29,135 square feet of space, the Glass House provides patrons the perfect vantage point to watch the river of traffic flowing beneath its span on the Will Rogers Turnpike.

2005, by which time there were only eight outlets left. By the spring of 2012, all were gone.

When the McDonald's Corporation was scouting Route 66 for new locations, they were no doubt thrilled to discover the building's integrated arches. It was a perfect location, and customers got a kick out of eating over the traffic. Beneath the bridge, some twenty-six thousand vehicles per day flow like a pair of rivers headed in opposite directions.

In 2013, the Glass House McDonald's abruptly shut down for much-needed renovations. It was showing its age, and the state wanted to revamp it as a showcase for people entering Oklahoma. "This is part of Oklahoma," said Tim Stewart, executive director of the Oklahoma Turnpike Authority, in *Tulsa World*. "This is part of history. We said, 'Okay, if we're going to preserve it, we want to make it outstanding.'"

At the time, many feared that the structure would never open again and that the integrity of the Interstate 44 landmark would fall by the wayside. Fears heightened after inspectors found asbestos that had to be removed. Worse, the archway bridge foundation was deteriorating.

After $15 million in repairs, the site reemerged in late 2014 as the Will Rogers Archway, still hosting the iconic McDonald's. Also

along for the ride were Oklahoma's Kum & Go convenience store and a Subway restaurant. Now a large seating area takes up the center space, along with some Will Rogers memorabilia. There's even a statue of a lasso-throwing Rogers that was once located outdoors.

Residents and Route 66 fanatics were delighted, but many were surprised to see one prominent feature—the legendary McDonald's name—removed from the building's exterior. Although the colors have been toned down, the grand arches remain as subtle reminders of the eatery's heritage.

ABOVE: The restored Glass House McDonald's is now called the Vinita Service Plaza. The famous golden arches fast-food joint is still a tenant but not the main part of the show.

RIGHT: The Vinita, Oklahoma, McDonald's is definitely a site worth visiting. The architecture is inspiring and the vantage point is unsurpassed for a roadside fast-food eatery.

6.
ELMER'S BOTTLE TREE RANCH

ORO GRANDE, CALIFORNIA

The Bottle Tree Ranch is a whimsical reminder that one man's trash is definitely another man's treasure. It all comes down to your priorities in life and how you look at things.

Though glass has served us for thousands of years, people still find ways to use it that excite our senses. A large part of glass's allure is its fragile nature: hit it with a hammer and it will break; drop it on the ground and it will shatter. Slip a message in a bottle and drop it in the ocean, and after decades of tumbling in the waves and sand, it's transformed. Hold it to the light and a new message returns— a singularity of art and utility.

If you're driving through the California desert on Route 66, it's a message that will surely seduce your gaze and compel you to stop. There, in the otherwise nondescript town of Oro Grande, thousands of trees have sprouted! But keep in mind there is no abundance of water here nor is this a desert oasis. Gleaming, reflective, and outright bedazzling, the "miracle" is man made, the result of a decades-long obsession with glass bottles and their light-bending properties.

This two-acre lot is Elmer Long's backyard, a come-as-you-please site that he created out of love for found objects. Like the magpie, which collects shiny objects to decorate its nest, Long, an eccentric known far and wide as "the Bottleman of Oro Grande," has handpicked thousands of discarded glass containers and installed them on metal frames. The bottles translate the energy of the hot desert sun into a colorful apparition that's as soothing to look at as it is fascinating to ponder.

The first question that comes to mind is why would anyone spend most of their life toiling in the desert to create such an attraction?

For Elmer Long, the question is multifaceted and revolves mostly around his childhood memories. When Long was just a kid, he would rather join his father on desert treasure hunts than play baseball. Together, they scoured the scorched landscape for the everyday items that other human beings discarded. In the process, father and son found each other.

The fact that the biggest and most popular road in the country passed by right out front didn't hurt. It was easy to amass the vast collection of discarded bottles and other junk that today make up Elmer's Bottle Tree Ranch. All Elmer and his dad had to do was wait, and the people passing by did the rest. Like seashells on an ocean beach, the treasures washed up: an empty Coke bottle here, a discarded tequila flask there, and maybe a green wine bottle or two.

When Long's father (also named Elmer) finally passed away, Elmer realized the number of bottles the pair had collected over the years was staggering. He wasn't sure what to do with the collection, but one thing was for certain: he wasn't going to throw away what amounted to a personal bond between him and his father. For Elmer, the bottles represented something beautiful. The only relevant question was how to showcase that beauty.

Artist Elmer Long's father took him to Manhattan Beach during the 1950s, where they picked through the garbage for treasures. Glass bottles became his object of fascination.

The answer came one day when Long began experimenting with a simple metal framework that looked a lot like a small tree. He started to decorate the skeleton with the colorful glass bottles, and suddenly a new entity came to life. What would become the basis for the ranch had reached out from another dimension and made itself known to the artist. Before long, most of the found objects, which included more than just bottles, found their way onto the metal trees: antlers, a saxophone, a traffic signal, antique rifles, a rusted tricycle, windmills, half a surfboard, a carousel horse, and more.

The Ranch is so engaging that locals and Route 66 fans alike have put considerable effort into keeping it around. Elmer Long is an artist doing work on his own land, and his work takes significant time, but art also takes funding. Visitors will notice a donation box to help Elmer keep his vision up and running. If you donate, you are more than welcome to help yourself to a sample of tumbled glass.

For some, that's just not enough. As strange as it may sound, many visitors want their very own Bottle Tree Ranch. "People come here and ask me to build them one. I won't do it," Long told the *Los Angeles Times* in 2011. "I've got no interest in money. I tell them, 'Build your own—there's my welding machine, you can use it.' How could it possibly mean anything to you if you don't make it yourself?"

ABOVE: Topped with found objects such as broken rifles, animal skulls, vintage fans, retro toys, old bells, and more, each one of Elmer's two hundred trees is a completely unique work of art.

OPPOSITE: Folk artist Elmer Long has created his own oasis for art in the California desert, all by hand. It's a place for contemplation and a free space to let your imagination soar.

TOP FIVE

WEIRD

to go and

WEIRD

to do

1 2 3 4 5

BOB'S GASOLINE ALLEY

822 Beamer Lane, Cuba, Missouri

Just off of old Route 66, Bob Mullen owns this outdoor extravaganza of service station signs and other gasoline station memorabilia and welcomes visitors daily. Known by aficionados as "petroliana," these artifacts from the golden age of full-service are a sight to behold.

COOL SPRINGS

8275 West Oatman Road, Kingman, Arizona

On the gradual climb up the Gold Hill Grade to Oatman, Arizona, lies a restored roadside treasure called the Cool Springs Camp. Back in 2001, Ned Leuchtner bought the property and restored the site to its former glory. Today, it's a gift shop and place to grab a snack.

DAIRY KING

100 North Main Street, Commerce, Oklahoma

Directly across the street from the Hole in the Wall Conoco, Dairy King is a snack shop housed in a vintage Marathon gas station building. Charles Duboise runs the place and makes signature "Route 66 cookies" that he has shipped to customers as far as Europe.

HACKBERRY STORE

11255 Arizona-66, Kingman, Arizona

The Hackberry Store is one of the icons of Arizona Route 66, a bonafide shrine to the highway. Although no gas is sold here, visitors have a wide variety of souvenirs to choose from. The place is packed with all the cool stuff you might imagine, including gas pumps and signs.

THE RUSTY BOLT

22345 West Route 66, Seligman, Arizona

The Rusty Bolt is known for its dummies—that is to say, the showroom mannequin type. Along with a 1959 Ford Edsel, they adorn the front facade, lounging about in all their glory, daring passersby to come on in and take part in this biker-bar turned tourist trap photo-op.

TALES OF THE INFAMOUS AND LEGENDARY

Let us pay tribute to the important pioneers, visionaries, and events that were responsible for the creation, promotion, and ultimate notoriety of Highway 66. From "Get Your Kicks" songwriting legend Bobby Troup to the so-called father of the highway, Cyrus Avery, and the unsung runners who burned up the pavement on foot, to the tragic connection with the Trail of Tears, here are the oft-overlooked histories of the people whose fates were so intertwined with the route John Steinbeck dubbed the "Mother Road."

1.
TROUP WAS THE TROUBADOUR OF 66

LOS ANGELES, CALIFORNIA

Using a simple twelve-bar blues arrangement, Troup's highway tribute quickly became the theme song for anyone and everyone making a motor trip via Route 66.

If one song comes to mind when you think of Route 66, it has to be the one penned by Bobby Troup. In writing "(Get Your Kicks on) Route 66," the jazz pianist and songwriter created a fun and upbeat mantra to a road known for adventure and memory-making. While he wrote numerous other tunes, this is the one that earned him musical immortality.

Troup was born in Harrisburg, Pennsylvania, on October 18, 1918, and grew up attending a boarding school. He graduated from the University of Pennsylvania with a degree in economics. When his military orders came through in January 1942, he went on to complete basic training and later helped recruit the country's first black marines.

While in the military, Troup served as a recreation officer. His efforts helped to establish a basketball court, recreation hall, mini golf course, and an outdoor boxing ring. He also helped to establish the first African American Marine Corps band. Troup's real love was music, and in his spare time, he liked nothing better than to write songs and play the piano.

While serving at Montford Point, North Carolina, Troup composed a song called "Take Me Away from Jacksonville." His fellow marines couldn't get enough, and it soon became an anthem for the installation, its popularity extending all the way to Camp Lejeune. He scored his first number-one hit in 1941 after Sammy Kaye and His Orchestra recorded the tune "Daddy."

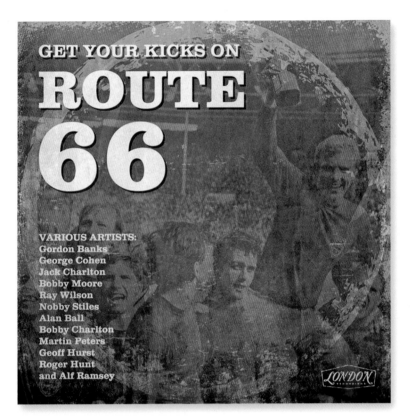

GET YOUR KICKS ON
ROUTE 66

VARIOUS ARTISTS:
Gordon Banks
George Cohen
Jack Charlton
Bobby Moore
Ray Wilson
Nobby Stiles
Alan Ball
Bobby Charlton
Martin Peters
Geoff Hurst
Roger Hunt
and Alf Ramsey

LONDON

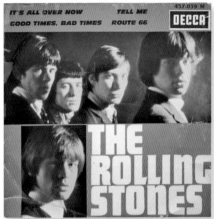

According to interviews, Troup got the initial inspiration for the Route 66 song while taking a cross-country road trip from Pennsylvania to the West Coast. He had a crazy idea that he wanted to become a famous Hollywood songwriter, so he packed up his bags (and his wife, Cynthia) and pointed the wheels of his 1941 Buick west. The first part of the journey started out on US 40, and, believe it or not, Troup almost wrote a song about that roadway!

However, once the couple made it out of the Midwest, Route 66 became a highlight of the trip. Suddenly, a wealth of material sparked Troup's muse. After Cynthia came up with the catchy title "(Get Your Kicks on) Route 66," the choice was clear. During the next ten days on the road, Troup penned the lyrics. Using gas station roadmaps collected along the way, he added finishing touches to the verses when they finally settled in their new Los Angeles digs.

Later, when the couple reviewed the song, it read like a fun-filled travel brochure showcasing towns and attractions along the way. Significant towns comprising the song's backbone were rattled off in catchy syncopation between other lyrics: Saint Louis, Joplin, Oklahoma City, Amarillo, Gallup, Flagstaff, Winona, Kingman, Barstow, and San Bernardino epitomized the look and feel of 66.

"(Get Your Kicks on) Route 66" was recorded by myriad artists, including Nat King Cole, Chuck Berry, the Rolling Stones, George Benson, and Depeche Mode.

LEFT: Troup tried his hand at acting and is well remembered for his portrayal of Doctor Joe Early on the 1970s television show *Emergency!*. His wife, Julie London, played nurse Dixie McCall.

OPPOSITE: Musicians who recorded cover versions of Troup's 66 anthem also include Asleep at the Wheel, Dr. Feelgood, and the King Cole Trio.

The only state not represented in the song was Kansas (with only eleven miles of road). The omission didn't matter in the grand scheme of things, though, and "(Get Your Kicks on) Route 66" went on to become a hit record. The first artist to gain notoriety with the song was crooner Nat King Cole (released as a 78-rpm record in 1946). His version hit the US R & B and pop charts at top speed and remains one of the most evocative renditions to this day.

Perry Como also recorded a version in 1959, followed by Chuck Berry in 1961. Berry put his unique spin on the song, electrifying it with his classic guitar riffs, a style that formed the basis of rock and roll. Whether it was unintentional or for comic effect, Berry was also the first artist to pronounce the city "Barstow" to rhyme with "cow."

After guitarist Keith Richards of the Rolling Stones heard the cover, he and Mick Jagger decided that they had to record the tune as well. Coming in at a radio-friendly recording time of 2:20, it appeared on their eponymous first album in 1964.

Troup went on to play Dr. Joe Early in the TV show *Emergency!* and followed many other pursuits, but none of them ever equaled the buzz that he generated with "(Get Your Kicks on) Route 66." He passed away in 1999, content in the fact that he did become the Hollywood songwriter of his dreams. In the process, he laid down the groovy soundtrack for a highway that would be known and loved by millions who planned to motor west.

2.
C. C. PYLE'S BUNION DERBY

CHICAGO, ILLINOIS

From the town of Claremore, Oklahoma, Andy Payne was a small-town boy without a big national sponsorship who won the famed Bunion Derby race.

The 1929 International Transcontinental Footrace, or "Bunion Derby," was one of the earliest American foot races, and as it happens, much of it was held on Route 66.

The year was 1929 when a field of 199 runners departed the starting line in Los Angeles to begin the long and grueling trek to New York City. After eighty-four days and 3,424 miles, only fifty-five runners crossed the finish line.

In those Depression-era days, it was unheard of to offer $25,000 in prize money, and the hefty reward attracted the interest of the national and international press. In fact, the very first mobile radio station in America was slated to cover the event in what might perhaps be considered the first ever reality-based program, painting a colorful canvas of sound by sharing both the runners' and viewers' perspectives.

However, the most interesting part of the race wasn't the big prize money or news media. While the majority of racers were Caucasian, 10 percent came from diverse backgrounds. Of the 199 runners entered, there were five African Americans, one Jamaican (from Canada), and fifteen Latinos, as well as American Indians and Pacific Islanders.

In an age defined by discrimination and segregation, how did organizers manage to host such a diverse event? Easy—through the

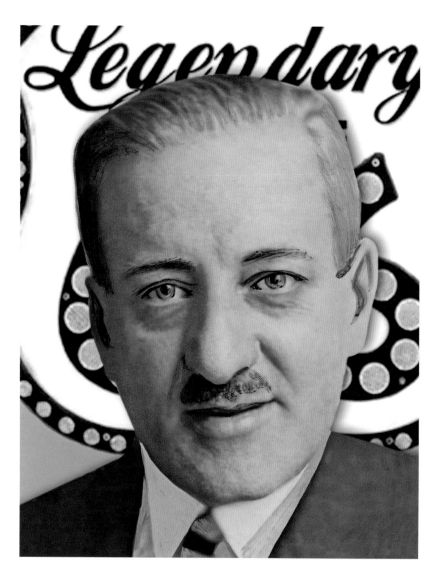

Legendary

efforts of none other than "Cash and Carry" Pyle, America's earliest sports promoter, a man who could sell an icebox to a penguin. To cover the expenses of meals and overnight sleeping camps, he negotiated carnival-like events in the race towns. Of course, every city had to pay a fee for hosting privileges.

When a young Oklahoma athlete by the name of Andy Payne first heard about the race, he immediately began plotting his participation. He had the running skills and always took first place in local events. But he needed some backing to enter the race, and his family was reluctant to devote scarce resources.

Through sheer determination, Payne won them over. With newfound confidence, he approached his local chamber of commerce for additional support and got them to donate another seventy-five dollars. With that and a loan from his father, he was off and running. Of course, he promised his

Pyle's nickname was "Cash and Carry." He was a theater owner from Champaign-Urbana, Illinois, and also the manager of football great Red Grange and tennis player Suzanne Lenglen.

PREVIOUS PAGE: C. C. Pyle's first annual Trans-American Footrace was the major event of 1928, one of the first to broadcast slice-of-life vignettes from various points along the route.

family that after he won, he would use the prize money to pay off the mortgage on the farm.

Payne wasted little time preparing for the race and started a strict long-distance training regimen. To make sure that he had the stamina to go the distance, Payne ran fifteen to thirty miles every day. In a few months, an average farm boy with little racing experience had acquired the moxie needed for the cross-country competition.

Still, the race posed significant challenges. First, the roadway was in bad shape for most of Route 66. Potholes were a menace to all the runners, and an uneven roadbed of dirt made it difficult to maintain a steady pace. The weather was an issue too. In the Mohave Desert, the thermometer pushed well past 95 degrees Fahrenheit. At night, it quickly swung to the other extreme, with freezing temperatures in the mountain passes. By the time the runners reached New Mexico, only half were left.

When the remaining contestants reached the state of Texas, they soon learned that they had more to worry about than road conditions and the weather. Here, it was the locals who slowed them down, most notably the Ku Klux Klan, which insisted that people of color were not welcome in the communal tent city that race planners had prepared for the night.

All non-white contestants had to sleep in a segregated tent; during the day they had to endure all manner of racial slurs and threats. In western Oklahoma, for example, it was reported that a farmer followed one of the African American runners and threatened to shoot him if he dared to pass a white contestant.

However, in the true spirit of sport, white runners stood up for their competitors. And along the route, the black community came out and supported them with food, water, and shelter. This helped even the playing field somewhat and allowed many minorities the chance to complete the race. Three of the top ten runners were people of color.

The final laps were run in New York City's Madison Square Garden. The winner? None other than Andy Payne, the young farm boy from Oklahoma.

Pyle signed Red Grange in 1925. Grange later became a star for the Chicago Bears of the National Football League. He also founded the first New York Yankees football team.

The Bunion Derby race began at the Legion Ascot Speedway in Los Angeles and finished in New York's Madison Square Garden. Payne won in 573 hours, 4 minutes, and 34 seconds.

3.
COURT JESTER OF ROUTE 66

OOLOGAH, OKLAHOMA

Known as "Oklahoma's Favorite Son," Will Rogers was not only a famous writer but also an actor and political commentator who came to represent the good will of Highway 66.

Of all the people who have called Oklahoma home over the centuries, perhaps the most influential have been American Indians. And the Osage and Cherokee of the area hold the man named William Penn Adair "Will" Rogers—a one-time circus performer, international film star, newspaper writer, and member of the Cherokee nation—in highest regard throughout Oklahoma and along the many miles of Route 66. At his zenith, Rogers was known as "Oklahoma's Famous Son."

Born in 1879 on the Dog Iron Ranch near the present-day town of Oologah, Oklahoma, Rogers was one of nine children. His father came to the area and settled the ranch in 1856; it eventually grew to more than sixty thousand acres. Both parents were of Cherokee descent. Mary America Schrimsher Rogers was from a long line of Cherokee royalty, and Clement Vann Rogers was a Cherokee nation senator who contributed to the Oklahoma Constitution. Although Rogers often referred to his Native American heritage in his comedy writings, it was an important part of his life.

Before his lucrative careers as a writer, comedian, vaudevillian, and actor, Rogers learned how to handle and rope cattle on the ranch, skills that later bolstered his cowboy image on the big screen. He would make the forty-mile trek on a cattle trail from Dog Iron Ranch to Willie Halsell College in Vinita, a section of trail that eventually became part of Route 66.

Rogers started his entertainment career as a trick roper in Texas Jack's Wild West Circus in South Africa. Later, he returned to the United States, and, after wrangling a steer that stormed the seats at

New York's Madison Square Garden, he broke into vaudeville with a rope-and-pony act. Rogers spent ten years perfecting his routine at a place called the Roof and at other venues in the city.

The Ziegfeld Follies came next, after which Rogers made his debut in silent films. His career took off from there, and he appeared in forty-eight silent films. When the talkies debuted, he continued acting and became a top star in the medium. Funny thing was, he always played himself in the films. He ad-libbed a good portion of his lines and somehow managed to interject some of his own political views into the dialog. His favorite director was John Ford, who would later become famous for his work on the film version of *The Grapes of Wrath*.

In many of his stage acts, Rogers told stories—not fictional tales, but monologues about the news of the day. "All I know is what I read in the papers" was one of his most famous lines, with the commentary that followed focused on current events and the state of the nation. Rogers had a particularly wry sense of humor and a knack for poking fun at all levels of society without offending anyone. He used this gift to question the many faults he saw in America from the common man's point of view. In doing so, he became the leading political wit.

Rogers translated his everyman viewpoint and ability to make off-the-cuff remarks to the newspapers, writing many popular articles and columns. From 1922 to 1935, Rogers had a popular syndicated column in the *New York Times*. In 1926, a short daily column called "Will Rogers Says" reached an audience of forty million readers. His work also appeared in the *Saturday Evening Post* on a regular basis.

ABOVE LEFT: Located in the town of Oologah, Oklahoma, the Dog Iron Ranch was the historic birthplace of famed humorist and writer Will Rogers. The family donated it to the state of Oklahoma.

ABOVE: In 1948, the US Postal Service issued a three-cent stamp in Rogers's honor, bearing one of his most famous sayings: "I never met a man I didn't like."

ABOVE: An expert roper and trick rider, Will Rogers started his career working the vaudeville circuit perfecting his cowboy act, Texas Jack's Wild West Circus. It was his first real gig.

OPPOSITE: Route 66's second name is the Will Rogers Highway. The Will Rogers Turnpike is the section of Interstate 44 between Tulsa, Oklahoma, and Joplin, Missouri.

Before his death in 1935 in an airplane crash in Alaska (an ill-fated flight with the famous aviator Wiley Post), Rogers had penned more than four thousand newspaper articles. His style won over the affection of the American people and many powerful politicians.

Growing up in Oklahoma, Rogers was more than familiar with many of the towns that Route 66 passed through. Over the years, he often highlighted Route 66 as America's most beloved roadway. He was such a vocal ambassador for the route that in 1952 the US Highway 66 Association unofficially co-named the road the Will Rogers Highway.

4.
FATHER OF THE HIGHWAY

TULSA, OKLAHOMA

Between the 1870s and the 1920s, the Good Roads Movement promoted the creation of better roads and highways across America, Route 66 included.

When we think about Route 66, we tend to focus on the iconic and historical nature of the road. What first comes to mind are the many millions of people who traveled down it, crossing the nation for business, recreation, or relocation. Fascinated with the physical trappings of the old road, we are ignorant of how it came about.

One thing is certain: US Route 66 didn't just appear overnight. While it began as a series of trails and disconnected roads, its ultimate existence is tied to a single man who saw into the distant future, assessed the needs of travelers, and took action.

That man was Cyrus Avery, the single most powerful driving force behind the now-historic highway. So strong was Avery's influence on the creation of Route 66 that by the time the road was paved completely from end to end, he was known to a good many as the "Father of Route 66." More than any other booster of highways in America, he made roads—and their improvement—the focus of his career.

Avery was born in Stevensville, Pennsylvania, on August 31, 1871, and his family made their living by farming. When he was ten years old, the family moved to Noel, Missouri, where he later went on to become a teacher. After earning a bachelor's degree, Avery married a woman named Essie McClelland, and they made Oklahoma City their home, where they would raise three children.

Before he focused on good roads, Avery tried his hand at several careers. At various times, he sold insurance, invested in the oil industry, and farmed. He was also a real estate investor and, as such,

UNITED STATES
SYSTEM OF HIGHWAYS
ADOPTED FOR UNIFORM MARKING BY THE
AMERICAN ASSOCIATION OF STATE
HIGHWAY OFFICIALS
NOVEMBER 11, 1926

was keenly aware that commerce required people to get from one place to another as quickly and efficiently as possible. This prompted his interest in road development and his membership in the Good Roads Movement of the early 1900s.

This group was a grassroots organization originally started by bicyclists during the 1870s. Before the automobile gained ubiquity, bicycles were all the rage. Aficionados who used them for travel, whether for long distances or short, were zealous in their demand for better roads.

As gas-powered vehicles shoved the bicycle to the wayside, the organization grew. With the ability to travel faster for longer distances, many more people became interested in the effort to fight for more roads and for existing roads to be improved. The higher speeds possible with automobiles demanded safer roads.

In 1913, Avery entered politics and became the commissioner of Tulsa, Oklahoma. He set out to make a positive difference in road development. His efforts helped spur the development of numerous projects, and he remained involved in groups such as the Ozark

Adopted for uniform marking by the American Association of State Highway Officials, Cyrus Avery's highway map outlined the road numbering system for 1926 and beyond.

Early roads were in great need of improvement, as seen in this Route 66 view taken near Ash Fork, Arizona. All it would take was time and a whole lot of taxpayer money.

Trail Association and the Associated Highways of America—early organizations that kept up and promoted trails throughout the states.

Avery furthered his mission when in 1924 the Oklahoma governor appointed him to the post of state highway commissioner. Only one year into the position, a pivotal event took place in his life and in the future life of Route 66: Avery was appointed to the federal board to develop a free, safe, and easily passable network of highways from one end of the country to the other. The group wanted the roads to be easy to follow so people didn't get lost, and there were to be no dead ends along the way.

Working with a small team of cartographers, the board began to map out where the first road would go, and Chicago to Los Angeles emerged as the top route. Originally, they named this road US 60, but a disagreement over the numbering broke out with the board's Kentucky delegates. Soon after, they settled on US 66 for its pleasing sound and, by some reports, favorable standing among numerologists. The rest, as they say, is history.

In 1927, Avery cofounded the US Highway Association with the mission of getting the end-to-end highway completely paved and promoting it. Boosters began touting Route 66 in print media, on maps, in travel brochures, and with staged events. America's Main Street was yet a toddler, gaining a strong foothold in the transportation infrastructure of the United States, but it was on its way.

ABOVE: Cyrus Avery pushed for the creation of the US Highway 66 Association in 1927 and, through it, promoted tourism on the route and rallied for it to be paved from end to end.

LEFT: Cyrus Avery and friends leave on an Ozark Trails road trip, a precursor to Route 66 that he helped create. The early network connected Saint Louis, Missouri, and Amarillo, Texas.

5.
JOHN STEINBECK'S
THE GRAPES OF WRATH

THE MOTHER ROAD, OKLAHOMA

Author John Steinbeck was immortalized in gold in 1984 when a coin was struck in his honor. The reverse side features a rural farm, much like the ones in the American Dust Bowl.

The Grapes of Wrath is a story of hardship and changing America. It also goes hand in hand with Route 66. Both are a testament to America's ingenuity, opportunity, and bootstrap mentality. The road is always the future, for we move forward on it, leaving the past behind as a fading memory that grows smaller in the rearview mirror with each passing mile.

The Grapes of Wrath was published in 1939, at the tail end of the Great Depression. Author John Steinbeck won the Pulitzer Prize for fiction and the National Book Award for the novel. Even today, it's widely acclaimed as a classic of American literature. Often taught as a companion to history lessons, it is a stark reminder of the hardships many Americans faced at the time, namely the ravages of climate change, mechanization of farming, and cruelty of fellow man.

As with many of Steinbeck's books, this title focused on poor, rural Americans. It was such a success because it evoked a true vision of the land that, at the time, was still fresh in Americans' minds. At the time of publication, the nation's middle class had been decimated and, with it, the very fabric of America torn asunder.

The story itself is a simple one, following the life of the Joad family, Oklahoma residents and honest, hard-working tenant farmers. In addition to the challenges of a dead economy, the Dust Bowl and the insurmountable drought conditions that it brought affected farming-dependent Midwestern regions. Starving and with no way to make a living at home, many "Okies" set out to seek a new land.

California boasted that it had available jobs, so down-and-out families such as the Joads packed up their jalopies with their personal belongings and headed west. From Texas, Oklahoma, Arkansas, Missouri, and Kansas they went, trickling over the feeder routes that connected to the highway at the center of it all: Route 66.

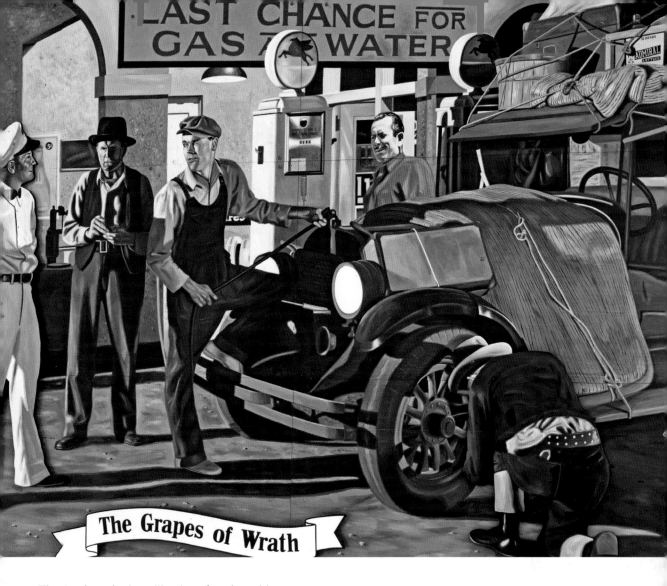

The Grapes of Wrath

The Joads and others like them faced troubles not uncommon to many Okies. Their crops had been completely decimated, and they were struggling to make a living. Their homes had been repossessed after they were unable to pay the bank loans.

Tom Joad was forced to make a choice. While he did not want to uproot his family, there was no way to make a living in Oklahoma. The only solution was to pack it all up and head to California on Highway 66.

While *The Grapes of Wrath* is steeped in symbolism, no symbol in the book quite surpasses that of the highway. While it is surely a symbol of new life and new possibilities, it becomes much more for the Joads. In Chapter 12, a part of the book almost completely dedicated to Route 66, Steinbeck first coins a new nickname for the road.

Depicting a scene from *The Grapes of Wrath* movie (with Steinbeck himself in a color cameo), this evocative tribute billboard was seen along a California Highway.

At the chapter open, Tom Joad plays observer and describes the exodus of the migrants:

> 66 is the path of a people in flight, refugees from dust and shrinking land, from the thunder of tractors and shrinking ownership, from the desert's slow northward invasion, from the twisting winds that howl up out of Texas, from the floods that bring no richness to the land and steal what little richness is there. From all these the people are in flight, and they come into 66 from the tributary side roads, from the wagon tracks and the rutted country roads. 66 is the mother road, the road of flight.

The chapter alternates between the road and worrying over various sounds coming from the engine or drivetrain, creating a palpable sense of tension for the reader. The automobile was like a lifeboat, but a fragile one. With little extra money and few places to make repairs, breaking down meant the end of the line. Indeed, Route 66 was littered with many abandoned jalopies . . . and broken dreams.

But the Joad family had to press on, and, as Ma Joad often said, "keep the family together." There was no turning back. The Mother Road was there to transport them to their new life, but it offered no special favors—at the end of the line, she birthed you into a harsh new world where it was your job to learn how to walk again and find your way.

Eventually, the Joads made it to the promised land of California, but the ending was more than bittersweet. Californians did not welcome the migrants with open arms, and the promise of jobs in the fields proved to be overblown. They had to work just as hard as they did in the towns they came from, if not harder, in a pre-welfare age when working for a living meant whether you had food on the table and a decent place to rest your head at night.

OPPOSITE: During the "dirty thirties," rollers such as this Texas panhandle monster would inundate an area with fine, choking dust, making farming, if not living, nearly impossible.

TOP: Steinbeck authored sixteen novels, and his Pulitzer Prize–winning *The Grapes of Wrath* (1939) is considered to be his masterpiece. In its first seventy-five years, it sold fourteen million copies.

ABOVE: Coins and candy are left in tribute at John Steinbeck's gravesite, located at the Garden of Memories Memorial Park, Salinas, California.

6.
ON THE TRAIL OF TEARS

INDIAN NATIONS, OKLAHOMA

GALLUP, NEW MEXICO
"the Indian Capital"

AUGUST
11·12·13·14
1949

INTER-TRIBAL
INDIAN *Ceremonial*

Very few of the happy travelers who get their kicks on Route 66 realize that part of the old road follows the path of what the Cherokee nation called *nu na da ul tsun yi*, or "the trail where they cried." In Missouri and Oklahoma, segments of this corridor crossed or coincided with the future alignment of America's Main Street. Along this path, thousands of American Indian men, women, and children were prodded westward by state militias and agents of the federal government.

It's horrifying to think that a road with such promise had its precursor in misery, but that's how it happened. The story unfolded during the early 1800s as the East Coast became more and more populated with white settlers and immigrants. Of course, these newcomers required more and more land. Someone had to move. According to many respected statesmen of the age, that someone was the so-called "savage" or "red man."

At the time, President Andrew Jackson saw progress through the lens of European culture and didn't believe that any advancement of the developing nation was possible as long as American Indians were in the picture.

Of course, greed played a large part as well. Gold was discovered on Cherokee land near Dahlonega, Georgia, in 1829, leading to the nation's second gold rush. With riches at stake, white people found it easy to disdain an entire culture for being different, whether that meant how or whom the other culture worshipped, the kind of clothes they wore, or the customs they cherished. Motivation to uproot the original inhabitants and relocate them was strong.

Gallup, New Mexico, was known as the "Indian Capital" during the glory days of Route 66. Back then, people came to see American Indians in their so-called natural environment.

Against this backdrop, Congress passed the Indian Removal Act in 1830, shamelessly laying the legal groundwork for the removal of thousands of Cherokee, Chickasaw, Choctaw, Muscogee, and Seminole people from their tribal lands in the American South. Overnight, lawmakers summarily extinguished the Indian title to lands. American law was crafted to give the usurper both the upper hand and legal precedence with no recourse for the loser, no matter that indigenous people had occupied the space for millennia.

Bureaucrats decided that "Indian territory" west of the Mississippi was a much better place for the tribes to live, and that's where the powers that be planned to resettle them. The tribes had no champion in the government, no means to stage a protest, and no one to hear complaints. The US military rounded up members of the Five Civilized Tribes living as autonomous nations and marched them off.

The exodus took place over a period of years, but it seemed that with each journey, the timing was always off. Weather extremes of hot and cold were not at all favorable, especially under the duress of being marched cross country. Ill-prepared, many died en route.

At Tulsa's Woolaroc Museum, Robert Lindneux's evocative portrayal of the Trail of Tears brings a forgotten event in American history out into the light for all to witness.

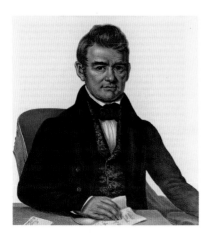

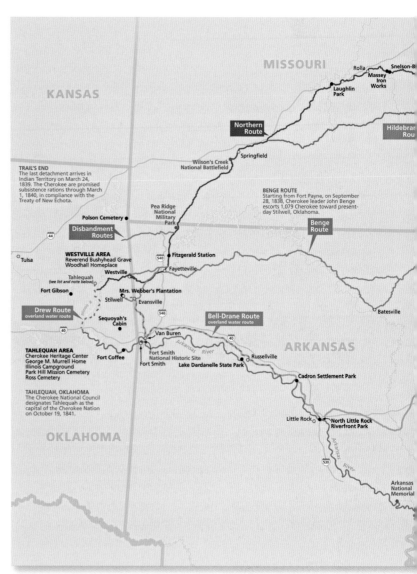

TOP: John Ross, a Cherokee Chief and legislator who led the Cherokee people west from Georgia upon their forced removal, circa 1836.

ABOVE: This brochure for Miami, Oklahoma, fails to mention the sordid past of the American Indian resettlement here, including the Trail of Tears that brought so much heartache and misery.

At the same time, the sicknesses of the white man did their part to decimate the numbers. Infectious diseases, such as whooping cough, dysentery, cholera, and typhus, consumed the normally healthy tribes, and the sick dropped dead where they were walking. Of the fifteen thousand Muscogee natives who started off on the ill-fated trek, nearly four thousand died. Of seventeen thousand Choctaw, six thousand were lost.

With so much cruelty and death at every turn, the Trail of Tears became a breeding ground for ghosts and restless spirits. It was as if the devil himself was riding herd ahead of the pack, as the trailhands in charge made sure that the flow of humanity continued, rolling the dead

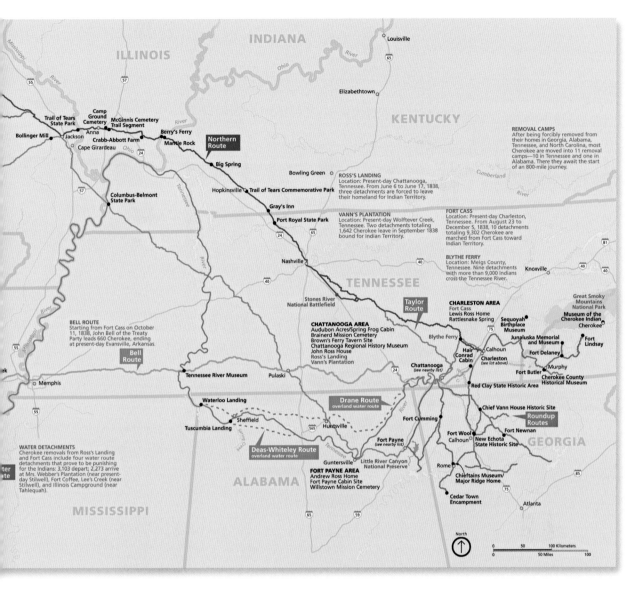

The infamous Trail of Tears wasn't just a single route but a combination of many paths and trips completed over a series of years that ended in the Oklahoma territories.

off the trail to keep things moving, allowing no time even to stop and dig a grave or pay one's last respects. The living fared no better: they teetered on the edge of death, starving and malnourished.

Eventually, some tribes ended up in Oklahoma but struggled to establish a foothold. Of those that relocated, only the Cherokee nation saw any resurgence in population. If Oklahoma Route 66 were to commemorate anyone, it should be the American Indians who made that horrible journey on the Trail of Tears—a sad chapter relegated to the backwaters of history.

TOP FIVE

WEIRD to go and WEIRD to do

1 2 3 4 5

66 DRIVE-IN THEATER

17231 Old 66 Boulevard, Carthage, Missouri

The 66 Drive-In theater is a must for all those retro-road enthusiasts who enjoy entertainment that can be seen right from the front seat of their automobile. Just pull in your vehicle, hook the speaker box to your window, and enjoy the show! Don't forget the popcorn.

MURAL CITY

Old Route 66, Cuba, Missouri

Known as the "Mural City," Cuba, Missouri, is one Route 66 town that is worth stopping to see—especially if you like colorful murals. Cuba was designated as the Route 66 Mural City by the Missouri legislature in recognition of Viva Cuba's Mural Project.

METEOR CITY TRADING POST

Route 66, Meteor City, Arizona

The Meteor City Trading Post once boasted the longest map of Route 66. Unfortunately, it was closed in 2012 and ransacked. It was recently purchased by a couple from Indiana who have high hopes to restore the site and make it a time capsule of Two Guns, Arizona.

SANDHILLS CURIOSITY SHOP

201 South Sheb Wooley Avenue, Erick, Oklahoma

The Sandhills Curiosity Shop is a store where nothing is for sale. Owners Harley and Annabelle, also known as the "mediocre musicmakers" ran the joint. Recent reports cite that the place has shut down, but the signs and other decorations are still available for photo ops.

TEE PEE CURIOS

924 East Tucumcari Boulevard, Tucumcari, New Mexico

Roadside kitsch is at its finest with this store's selection of some of the best doo-dads you will find along the old historic 66. It also happens to be the only teepee that is located directly on 66 itself, so be sure to stop in for some trinkets or to snap some photographs.

121

ROADSIDE TRIBUTES AND OTHER MONUMENTS

Strange creatures inhabit the Mother Road—roadside colossi of every shape and size. Along one stretch of road, outer space giants battle for dominance with ax-wielding lumberjacks, while on other parts of the route blue whale behemoths sit quietly, with Indian-themed totem poles marking the way. Meanwhile, mysterious monoliths and commemorative statues mark the way, much to the delight of the tourists who drive by to witness the wonders.

1.
GALLOWAY'S ROUTE 66 TOTEM POLES

FOYIL, OKLAHOMA

Foyil's Totem Pole park consists of eleven main sculptural objects. This bird-themed sculpture features an owl on one side and a woodpecker on the reverse.

Nathan Edward Galloway was one of the unsung creative geniuses of Route 66. His day job was as an industrial arts instructor for the Charles Page Home for Widows and Orphans in Sand Springs, Oklahoma. For twenty-two years, he taught others how to make things. For fun, he created bas relief portraits of former presidents and carved whimsical animal sculptures out of wood.

When it came to working with organic materials, Galloway was an artisan. A self-taught luthier, his skills allowed him to dabble in the realm of violins too, building "fiddles" that were serious musical instruments. He often said, "The way to open doors for people is to make them something." He proved it by gifting his priceless, one-of-a-kind art objects to friends and acquaintances.

It all started on some acreage Galloway owned outside of Foyil, Oklahoma, just off old Route 66. He spent the weekends there, building a future home for retirement. Copying the precision of his woodworking projects, he cut stones by hand and fitted them together to build the walls for a house. For six years, he pieced the home together, and in 1938, the project was complete.

There was one small catch: Galloway discovered that he couldn't sit still. His brain overflowed with myriad ideas that demanded attention. There could be no rest until he at least tried to finish a few of them.

For his first project, he chose something that had been on his mind for years: a totem pole. Most people in Oklahoma knew nothing about these mysterious monoliths, because it was mostly the indigenous cultures of the Great Northwest that made and used them to record stories. Some totem poles represented important events in a clan's history, others recorded a family's lineage, and some marked the great exploits of familiar legends. Because the trunk of even the tallest tree was finite in length (western red cedar was often used), the amount of information that even the most skilled artisan could hope to add was limited. Galloway appreciated this limited format and was energized by the idea that only the most important icons would fit.

To avoid weathering and decay, he decided to make his totem pole out of concrete and stone, which meant the project proved more strenuous than Galloway imagined. First, he constructed a metal framework, in the process using some six tons of wire and metal. Next came the cement, a total of twenty-eight tons, carefully applied to the framework by hand. Then, there were the one hundred tons of sand and rock he dredged from a nearby creek. The strange—if not unbelievable—part about his efforts was that the only container he used to move these materials was a five-gallon bucket!

After working with the mortar for a few weeks, he realized that his unique "carving" method called for special tools. It was easy to slap on the concrete, but bringing to life the detailed motifs required a little more precision. With no time to waste, nor extra money to spend, Galloway designed his own instruments from scrap metal and wood.

Sculpting the turtle at the base of the monolith was easy, but the more complex reliefs at the top required more daring. As the design reached upward to ninety feet, it became more and more dangerous to work on. To help him reach those heights, Galloway built a scaffolding and pulley system to hoist himself skyward.

In spite of his ingenuity, one man could do only so much. After eleven years of labor, the nine-story totem pole was finished. On the exterior, two hundred bas relief images painted in a rainbow of bright colors called out for people to decipher them. A tribute to our

Decorated with a variety of symbols, the arrowhead totem was constructed circa 1955 and continues the park's overall tribute to American Indians.

indigenous predecessors, the sculpture includes American Indian chiefs, mythical raptors, flowers, fanciful fish, and other symbols. Inside the tapered spire, evocative murals highlight memorable historical events.

Pleased with his creation, Galloway continued building. An Indian Hogan came next. He called it the "fiddle house" and used it to house and display the three hundred fiddles he carved over the years (each from a different type of wood). He crafted a whimsical roadside table for visitors too. Later, a huge arrowhead with a weathervane stuck on top of it joined the strange menagerie of concrete creatures. More sculptures were planned but never built—Galloway had many ideas but not enough time.

ABOVE: The Rogers County Historical Society—in concert with the Kansas Grassroots Arts Association—restored the totem poles to their original splendor between 1988 and 1998.

ABOVE RIGHT: Covered with a thin veneer of concrete, the main totem pole is made from red sandstone and framed with a steel and wood skeleton. It rests on a turtle base.

RIGHT: While it's obvious that Totem Pole Park pays homage to American Indians, it's interesting to note that none of the Oklahoma nations has a major tradition involving totem poles.

OPPOSITE: Ed Galloway sculpted his totem poles with images of birds, reptiles, and American Indians of the Northwest coast, Alaska, and Plains cultures.

2.
STANDIN' ON A CORNER...

WINSLOW, ARIZONA

The iconic Standin' on the Corner statue of a 1960s troubadour musician is only a few feet from a statue of Glenn Frey, cowriter of "Take It Easy" and member of the Eagles.

The city of Winslow, Arizona, reaped the bounty of Route 66 for decades. Like a horn of plenty, the Mother Road provided a seemingly endless supply of tourists and travelers. The curious rolled in from the east and west with cash in hand, and eager to experience the Southwest's "Indian country," dine at the last Harvey House, and marvel at the grandeur of Meteor Crater, the Painted Desert, and the Petrified Forest.

But as this former Atchison, Topeka, and Santa Fe Railway town soon learned, the gravy train always ends. The road went dark at the end of 1977 when the Route 66 traffic that used to run directly through the city was rerouted. It was as if someone had turned off the spigot controlling the flow of cars. "Progress" had bypassed Winslow, and the multilane path called Interstate 40 replaced all of Route 66 in the state of Arizona.

For the next thirteen years, Winslow joined hundreds of other doomed cities, helpless to improve its fate. Across Route 66's eight states and three time zones, tourism withered. Cities made valiant efforts to reinvent themselves, but it was pointless. One by one, businesses along America's Main Street boarded up windows and hung "Closed" signs. Only a miracle could restore business to the level that Route 66 once provided.

But Route 66 was a pugnacious fighter and refused to stay down. In 1990, people saw the very first signs of life when author Michael Wallis published his seminal volume *Route 66: The Mother Road*. Suddenly, the little green dot on the EKG screen blipped, if ever so slightly. More books, films, and events followed. Eventually there was

a groundswell of interest in Route 66, not just as a road that was used to get somewhere else, but as a destination in and of itself.

By the mid-1990s, the nostalgia for bygone America that had started small had grown into a juggernaut. Soon tourists from all walks of life and nations around the world embarked on a search for a lost America and a simpler time. Meanwhile, the faithful hit the pavement and raised money as historical groups started the task of rebuilding and restoring. Tourism grew, and the towns that were ready for it embraced the renaissance.

In 1999, Winslow furthered the effort to significant effect when they created Standin' on the Corner Park, a quiet place of reflection inspired by the Eagles' famous country-rock classic, "Take It Easy." Written primarily by Jackson Browne, the song told the tale of a young man's brief encounter with a woman passing by in a pickup truck. Browne wrote the lyric, "Well, I'm standin' on a corner / In Winslow, Arizona," but ran into a bit of writer's block. Glenn Frey, one of the founding members of the Eagles, played around with it and added, "Such a fine sight to see / It's a girl, my Lord / In a flatbed Ford / Slowin' down to take a look at me."

The collaboration proved fruitful, and the rest of the song practically wrote itself. Not surprisingly, "Take It Easy" was picked for the opening track on what was to be the band's eponymous first album. Although it only made it to number twelve on the *Billboard* charts, it eventually made the Rock and Roll Hall of Fame's list of top five hundred songs that helped shape America.

Back in the early 1910s, without access by Route 66, Winslow was an Arizona town that was not easily reached by cross-country automobile travel.

TOP: By the 1950s, Winslow had become one of the major stops along America's Main Street. Route 66 and the business of tourism was booming in America.

ABOVE: The famous song was written by Jackson Browne and Glenn Frey and was the band's first single. In 1972, it peaked at number twelve on the *Billboard* Hot 100 chart.

After countless plays on top forty radio, Winslow became ingrained in a generation's consciousness. People had a reason to visit and tangibly connect with the band that they loved so much. The fantasy is all there: the famous corner, a mural dedicated to the song, and even a flatbed Ford pickup truck, curbside. Where's the mysterious gal who shot the look? Check out the painted windows above and wave.

In September 2016, a bronze statue honoring Glenn Frey, who sang lead vocals on the song, was installed at the Standin' on the Corner Park. Depicting Frey during his younger days, the lifelike statue cost $22,000. Sadly, Frey never got to see it. He passed away in January of the same year at age sixty-seven.

The devotion to the song, adoration for the Eagles, and allegiance to Route 66 have formed a potent nexus of pop culture. Every year, more than one hundred thousand visitors come to Winslow to experience the magic for themselves. As the song spills out from the many car radios and souvenir shops, it's inevitable that you'll see someone standing on the corner recounting their youthful longing for love and that never-ending search for their soulmate.

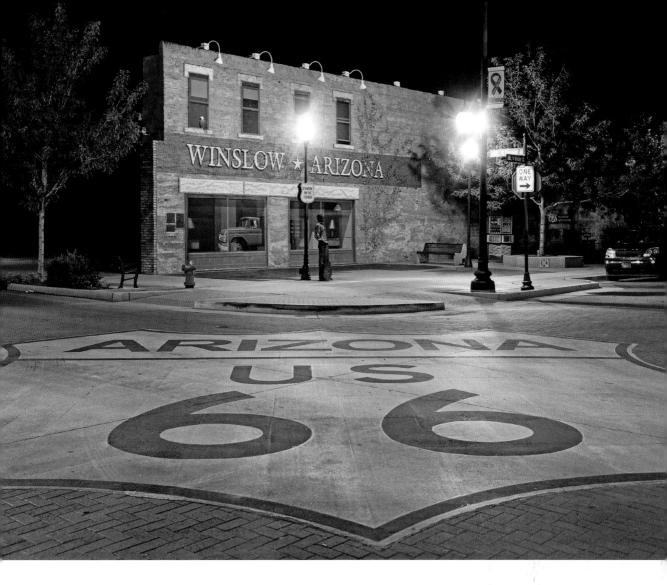

ABOVE: The song first debuted in 1972, but it took almost three decades to capitalize on the connection. Today, the corner sees almost one hundred thousand visitors per year.

RIGHT: The park contains a two-story trompe l'œil mural by John Pugh and a bronze statue by Ron Adamson. Of course, there's a red flatbed Ford parked just nearby.

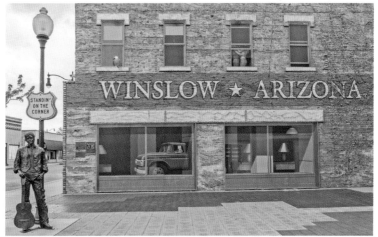

ROADSIDE TRIBUTES AND OTHER MONUMENTS **131**

3.
LUMBERJACKS AND SPACEMEN

FLAGSTAFF, ARIZONA

The Lumberjack Cafe of Flagstaff, Arizona, is home to this colorful Paul Bunyan variant. Note the hand positions that originally cradled a muffler.

There are giants among us in plain view, disguised in various shapes and sizes. Having served the human race for more than five decades, they are being toppled, discarded, and removed, trucked off to the local landfill like so many other unwanted advertising mascots of a forgotten age. Their mission was great: to serve us by getting the attention of passing motorists and amuse us with whimsy.

The story of these colossi began in 1961 when a man named Bob Prewitt was toying with the idea of building a lightweight horse trailer of fiberglass. He was a rodeo cowboy who was known for his roping and bulldogging, not for his trailer-making. Not one of his bronc-busting friends believed that the hitch he designed could hold one horse, much less two. To prove them wrong, he decided to craft two fiberglass horses to demonstrate his trailer's capabilities. His invention worked! Skeptics became believers, and Prewitt was in business.

Before long, word got around that he was a top fiberglass wrangler. One day, he got a call from the PB Café of Flagstaff, Arizona, a restaurant doing business along Route 66. Their request was a rather odd one, but not impossible to satisfy: "We need a twenty-foot-tall Paul Bunyan, ax and all." Prewitt was happy to oblige, creating the original mold that would one day be used to make all the restaurant's other roadside giants, which became known as "muffler men."

Prewitt had no idea that he gave birth to something that would one day become an icon of roadside America and Route 66. However, there was one thing he *did* know: he could earn a living by making fiberglass animals. He had a knack for it, and it was a lot less punishing on his body than bouncing up and down on a horse. Prewitt quit his rodeo gig and started up Prewitt Fiberglass Animals.

As crafted creatures of all shapes and sizes were created in his workshop, the Paul Bunyan mold lay forgotten. Then, in 1963, Steve Dashew of International Fiberglass came along and revived him. He had an idea that the giant figure had enormous untapped marketing potential, so he tracked down Prewitt and purchased the mold. At the time, fiberglass boats were Dashew's specialty, but he dropped the boat-building angle and switched to larger-than-life roadside statues.

As it turned out, the Paul Bunyan mold was very versatile: paint on a beard and you had a lumberjack; strap on a new chest and you had an Indian; bolt on a helmet and, *voila*, a spaceman. In all cases, these giants had one thing in common: the positions of their hands. If the statue has a right palm facing up and a left palm facing down (in its original

Labeled "Second Amendment Cowboy," this Glenn Goode variant once advertised an Amarillo barbecue steakhouse but was auctioned in 2014 to an RV park east of Cadillac Ranch.

ABOVE LEFT: At Bunyon's Restaurant in Cicero, Illinois, a former muffler man has been repurposed to sell hot dogs. Today, he cradles a bun and dog combo (note the awkward left-hand position).

ABOVE RIGHT: This seventy-five-foot-tall roadside giant weighs in at 43,500 pounds and is the fifth-largest statue in the United States. It was built in 1952 by the Mid-Continent Supply Company for the International Petroleum Exposition.

configuration, the Paul Bunyan mold held an ax horizontally), you can bet your pink slip it's a classic muffler man.

Dashew supplied these towering titans to small businesses everywhere, and they soon found special places in the hearts and minds of motorists. The timing was right. Big companies that wanted to capture more of the motorist market share fell head over heels for his giants too.

It began with Texaco's "Big Friends" ad campaign and an entirely new set of molds. The resulting giant featured a left arm raised in a "hello" wave and a right palm facing up. Soon, Dashew was making immense advertising mascots for oil companies, such as Phillips, Texaco, and ENCO. He even made dinosaurs for Sinclair. Other mutant muffler men—and women—followed, including the giantess Uniroyal Gal. Believe it or not, the fetching fiberglass femme fatale came with a removable dress and a painted bikini underneath!

Indeed, you could say they "broke the mold" when they made the original muffler men—the summer of 1976 saw the destruction of the original forms that gave them life. While one or two companies are attempting to keep the giant genre alive, the remaining statues are the last of the originals, facing extinction, waving a friendly goodbye to passing motorists . . . with one palm up, the other down.

ABOVE: Dressed for success, the Tastee Tree giantess is one of the few female roadside colossi that remain, hawking frozen treats along the roadside in the town of Madison, Illinois.

RIGHT: The Gemini Giant is one of the most familiar of Route 66 muffler men, a 1960s model standing sentry (perhaps for the arrival of aliens) in the quiet town of Wilmington, Illinois.

4.
GIGANTICUS HEADICUS

ANTARES, ARIZONA

A giant sleeps in the red sands of Antares, Arizona. There, along the Route 66 roadside, sitting quite serenely and seemingly without a care in the world, lives a Tiki-inspired giant resembling many of the things that pop culture fanatics go wild for. This oversized homage to the mysterious statues of Easter Island may not be grinning widely, but he's likely the most welcoming face you'll encounter along this stretch of Route 66.

Officially, he's called "Giganticus Headicus," a somewhat sarcastic, quasi-scientific moniker that strikes a tone as deadpan as the sculpture's visage. No, the big noggin wasn't transported here by ancient aliens or flown in by the occupants of mysterious black helicopters.

In fact, the enormous sculpture is art, somewhere in the realm of American pop. The art piece is the brainchild—or in this case, the brain bucket—of former New Jersey resident and artist Gregg Arnold. He got the idea to build his strange fourteen-foot melon in 2004, after reading the biographical diaries of famous New York pop artist Andy Warhol. Arnold was inspired and decided that he would try his hand at some art too.

Unfortunately, New Jersey was hardly the proper venue to debut something so kitschy as Giganticus Headicus, so Gregg began his search for an appropriate location. After poring over Google Earth, delving into a plethora of books on roadside America, and consulting top-secret maps of Area 51, he concluded that Route 66 was the best location to inspire his muse.

Giganticus Headicus currently lives on the northeast corner of Route 66 and Antares Road, only seventeen miles north of Interstate 40's popular Exit 53. The town of Antares was settled in the late 1800s after two railroads made their way through the land. They were stuck on how to get over the nearby mountains and opted to go around them instead. Later, Route 66 followed the same route, and the town flourished.

Interestingly, Antares takes its name from a star in the Scorpio constellation. The name is the Greek word for "rival of Mars" and refers to the star's red hues. Likewise, the town Antares was named for its bright, red sands—the same sands from which the bright teal Giganticus Headicus juts.

The structure is set up on what used to be the Kozy Korner trailer court, positioned directly in front of an oddly shaped triangular building that for a while languished in disrepair. For construction, Arnold used wood, metal, cement, chicken wire, and the universal pop artist's sculpting medium: Styrofoam.

With its large proboscis, Giganticus Headicus is a photo magnet for tourists, especially creative ones who like to stage "fun" pictures. Of course, the hands-down favorite is when visitors photograph friends and family "digging for gold" deep in one of old Headicus's giant nostrils.

Although the head is the most popular part of the exhibit, it's not Gregg Arnold's only creation. A whimsical pineapple seat accompanies the head, handy for taking a load off. There's also a

Created in 2004 by artist Gregg Arnold, Giganticus Headicus is a half-buried, fourteen-foot-tall pseudo-tiki sculpture crafted of metal, wood, chicken wire, Styrofoam, and cement.

GIGTICUS
HADICUS

windmill made from 1950s furniture, some funky robots, and even a "baby rattler" pit. But don't be put off if you're afraid of snakes: it's only a pit filled with harmless baby rattles.

A local group whose business was to look after the nearby caverns decided to work with Arnold to turn Giganticus Headicus and the Kozy Korner into the Antares visitor center. The deal was that Arnold could keep his artwork there (and add to it) while the central part of the building functioned as a visitor's center to help tourists explore everything Antares has to offer.

As for Giganticus Headicus? He greets people as they walk in. Some even walk out with a souvenir from Headicus's own section in the gift shop. In fact, he even has his own YouTube channel that plays psychedelic music and showcases the many photos of his bigness gathered from all corners of the internet.

ABOVE: Welcome to Antares, Arizona. After thirteen years of effort, artist Gregg Arnold has transformed this former RV park office into a gift shop and Route 66 visitors' center.

OPPOSITE: The sculpture has become one of the new photo-op stops along Route 66, and you can buy replicas of the crazy statue head in the onsite gift shop.

5.
CYRUS AVERY CENTENNIAL PLAZA

TULSA, OKLAHOMA

The *East Meets West* statue is an amazing tribute to Cyrus Avery, part of the Cyrus Avery Centennial Plaza located just off downtown Tulsa on old Route 66.

In 2003, the town of Tulsa, Oklahoma, kicked off an ambitious initiative known as Vision 2025. The revitalization plan called for a one-cent, thirteen-year sales tax increase, with funds generated slated to go toward economic development—specifically, the strengthening of adjacent neighborhoods and the promotion of tourism. Because twenty-six miles of Route 66 meandered through town, the city saw fit to allocate $15 million to improve the sites and structures relating to the national icon.

The improvements began along 11th Street from 193rd East Avenue, followed 11th Street west of Southwest Boulevard to Old Sapulpa Road, and finally ended at the Tulsa County line. Within this zone, many Route 66 landmarks were in a state of decline but worth saving. The revitalization turned the area into what some describe as an "outdoor museum," complete with statues, kiosks, stamped concrete, and historic markers—all easily viewable by car.

The first big project completed under Vision 2025 was the Cyrus Avery Centennial Plaza on Southwest Boulevard at Riverside Drive. It was funded in part by a grant from the Oklahoma Centennial Commission and was completed in 2008.

The U-shaped plaza, a fitting tribute to Avery and Route 66, is a Route 66 destination in its own right. The scene here evokes serenity despite the urban setting. Most striking is the intricately bricked walking surface that meets up with a garden of eight flagpoles that rise out of the plaza, one for each of the eight states through which the historic highway passes.

Above, a walking bridge with an exposed skeleton—known as the Route 66 Skywalk—allows pedestrians to pass safely over the busy Southwest Boulevard. The bridge is constructed in a dramatic arched design and caps the site's stature as a 66 landmark worth a look.

Mounted on both sides of the walkway, a Route 66 shield identifies the historic highway, with the city name mounted directly

Dedicated to the "Father of Route 66," the Cyrus Avery Centennial Plaza is a part of Tulsa's Vision 2025 development plan, which includes many historic Route 66 sites.

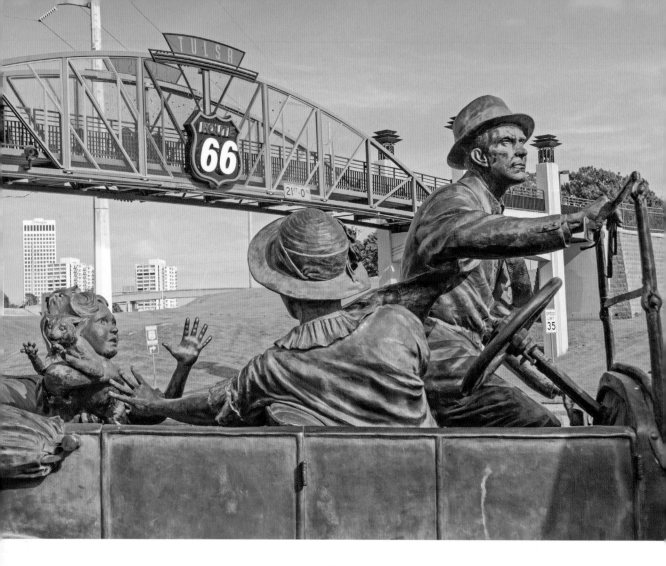

Texas artist Robert Summers imbued *East Meets West* with plenty of details, including a smashed grasshopper stuck to the front grill of the Ford and a key in the ignition.

above at the top of the arch. The general appearance of the shield bears a strong resemblance to the actual Phillips 66 logo, leading some to wonder if the oil concern had any influence on the design.

The plaza centerfield is occupied by *East Meets West*, a cast-bronze statue dedicated to Cyrus Avery in 2012. The setup consists of two main pieces, one that depicts a horse-drawn wagon (full of barrels of oil from the West Tulsa oilfields) and another showing Avery and his family in a Ford Model T.

According to the sculpture backstory, the horseless carriage in the diorama met up with and then startled the horse team. It's a fitting metaphor that portends the end of the horse-drawn age and the dawn of gasoline-powered transportation. Highways such as Route 66 transported America from an agrarian society to one on the cutting edge of technology.

The bronze sculptures are where the artists and planners behind the plaza exceeded all expectations. Texas artist Robert Summers imbued the statues with plenty of intricate details, from a smashed grasshopper stuck to the front grill of the Ford flivver to the key in the ignition. At 135 percent actual size, the sculpture weighs in at nearly twenty thousand pounds and stretches more than sixty feet from end to end, rising fifteen feet in the air.

Creating and assembling the piece was a challenge and took more than six years to finish. "It is a huge undertaking," said Clint Howard, Deep in the Heart Art Foundry director, during a phone interview from Bastrop, Texas, with the *Tulsa World* newspaper. "And it's fun. But still, it has been intimidating at times because we want everything to look perfect."

The unveiling was attended by hundreds of local townsfolk, including the plaza namesake's grandsons. The city of Tulsa and the family couldn't be prouder.

The Centennial Plaza walkway is a bridge spanning the old cut of Route 66, connecting the new plaza to a larger parking area directly across the street.

6.
THERE'S A BLUE WHALE IN PORT

CATOOSA, OKLAHOMA

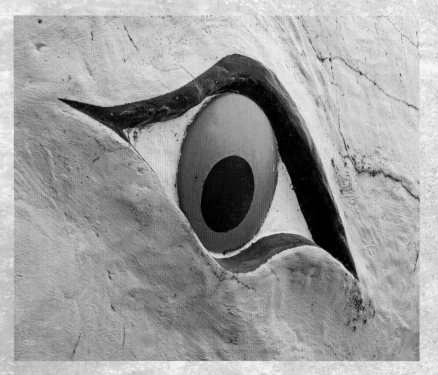

In an age devoid of theme parks and extreme attractions, the Blue Whale and its small adjoining pond became a popular swimming hole and roadside park.

Few people associate whales with heartland America. In fact, from the Port of Catoosa, Oklahoma, one could float all the way to the ocean's brine by way of the Verdigris, Arkansas, and Mississippi rivers. However, while no reports of *live* whales have been reported in this Rogers County seaport, this just so happens to be the part of Oklahoma where Route 66, the nurturing matriarch of dreams and ambitions, passes through. And here, just southeast of the river junction, you *will* find a whale smiling coyly from the roadside as if to say, "Look at me. I've made it."

Meet the Blue Whale of Catoosa, a gift from a husband to a wife that over the years has turned into a much-adored roadside attraction and Route 66 icon.

The story of the Blue Whale of Catoosa, or "Blue" as many of the locals call it, began back in the 1950s with a man by the name of Hugh Davis. He was an ardent zoologist and at one time head of the Tulsa Zoo. He was fortunate—his wife, Zelta, shared his interest in slithering reptiles.

Much in the tradition of lovers performing grand gestures, Hugh wanted to do something for Zelta that would stand throughout

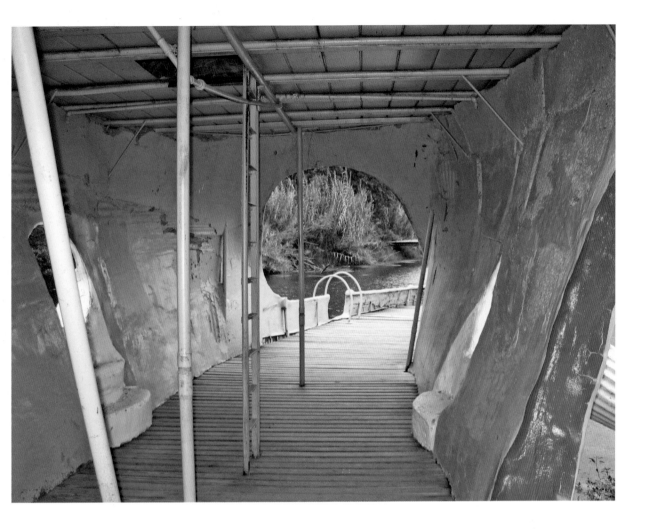

the decades as a testament to his love. Inspired by her penchant for collecting whale figurines, he got the idea to secretly construct a larger-than-life whale for her and present it to her on their anniversary.

He strategically positioned the whale next to a spring-fed pond on land the couple owned along Route 66. Hugh even expanded the tiny body of water so it was large enough for a swimming hole. When the day came for the reveal, Zelta loved everything about it, including the shape, color, and whimsical representation.

Of course, traffic passing by on Highway 66 couldn't ignore the smiling whale, and many stopped to see what it was. Eventually, Hugh opened the spot to the public as a small recreational park called Nature's Acres. He hired lifeguards and trucked in tons of sand to make the shores friendlier on bathers' feet. With the addition of picnic tables, the park had everything needed to keep visitors entertained all day.

Hugh Davis built the whale as a surprise for his wife, Zelta. The resulting structure grew into a roadside attraction and later an icon of Highway 66 travel.

ABOVE: Zelta Davis, the wife of the Blue Whale's designer, once wrangled alligators in her spare time as part of the onsite Animal Reptile Kingdom.

ABOVE RIGHT: Hugh Davis was the director of the Tulsa Zoo for thirty-eight years. He often brought sick animals home and nursed them back to health—when he wasn't milking rattlesnakes.

Hugh made the attraction even more exciting by adding a small zoo called the Animal Reptile Kingdom (ARK) next door. The herpetarium was shaped to look like Noah's ark; inside were snakes, lizards, turtles, crocodiles, and myriad other creatures.

Eventually, time caught up with Hugh and Zelta, and in 1988 they retired from the roadside attraction business. It was just too much work to feed the reptiles they housed and perform the daily upkeep of the park. Sadly, ARK fell into disrepair, but for some reason, time and age didn't affect the big blue whale.

Hugh Davis passed away in 1990, followed by Zelta in 2001, two more Route 66 originals gone. But the story of the blue whale was not finished. Later, Catoosa organized with employees of Hampton Inn to bring Blue and the park back to their glory days. Locals raised funds and initiated repairs. Volunteers restored Blue's sky-blue exterior to its original splendor. Somewhere, Zelta was smiling.

So, take a moment to grin at Blue as you trek down Route 66 and it will surely flash a grin right back. Leave it a message on its very own

Facebook page, or feel free to buy a Blue T-shirt at the stand that was erected next door to the town's most famous resident so you can take a little Blue with you wherever you go.

Although the tiny pond is no longer suitable for swimming, it's the perfect backdrop for a picnic on a sunny Oklahoma day. After all, what could be more fun than having lunch at one of *Time* magazine's top fifty roadside attractions? Just remember that Blue's whale-size eyes are watching, so make sure you're chowing down on ham and cheese and not a fish sandwich!

When compared to the mega waterslide parks of today, the Blue Whale's waterslide seems tiny in comparison. Yet it still entertained kids.

TOP FIVE

WEIRD to go and WEIRD to do

1 2 3 4 5

THE BUGG RANCH

Interstate 40, Conway, TX

The Bugg Ranch was created in 2002 as an advertising gimmick for a corporate travel plaza and is one of the rivals of the nearby Cadillac Ranch. Including five Volkswagen slug bug car wrecks planted head first into the ground, it's become a popular landmark along Route 66.

COPPER CART MOTORPORIUM

127 Route 66, Seligman, Arizona

Once a famous restaurant, this site now houses John Balistreri's Motorporium. With twenty-one motorcycles on display and a handful of cars, it's a bona fide museum, but Balistreri won't officially call it that until the number of vehicles on display reaches forty.

ELK CITY 66 SIGN

Old Highway 66, Elk City, Oklahoma

As part of the National Route 66 Museum in Elk City, Oklahoma, this gargantuan Route 66 sign is hailed as the largest in existence. It's a great stopping place to catch up on Route 66 history (the entire route, not just Oklahoma) and take some snapshots.

THE JACK RABBIT TRADING POST

US Route 66, Joseph City, Arizona

The Jack Rabbit Trading Post is a convenience store and curio shop most remembered for its mascot, a large fiberglass jackrabbit. "Here it is!" is their slogan, and you won't be disappointed when you reach this highway icon five miles west of Joseph City, Arizona.

WORLD'S 2ND LARGEST ROCKER

5957 Highway ZZ, Fanning, Missouri

Danny Sanazaro came up with the idea of building the world's largest rocking chair, although today it's called the Red Rocker. At forty-two feet, four inches high on rockers and thirty-one feet, six inches long, the steel pipe behemoth weighs 27,500 pounds and has now taken the place as the second largest.

EXEMPLARY EATS AND ROADSIDE TREATS

Exemplary Eats and Roadside Treats peels back the aluminum foil on the more unusual places to grab a bite to eat along the lunch counter of America's Main Street. Whether you're busting your gut for a free dinner by trying to wolf down 72 ounces of steak with all the fixings, feasting on Hatch Chile Hamburgers in Albuquerque, New Mexico, or chowing down on classic Cozy Dogs in Illinois, there's no denying that Route 66 offers a culinary cornucopia of offbeat eats.

1.
WORLD'S LARGEST KETCHUP BOTTLE

COLLINSVILLE, ILLINOIS

America's Largest Selling TANGY Catsup

Brooks OLD ORIGINAL CATSUP

Customers will travel far, if necessary, to get Brooks Old Original Catsup. It's that distinctive...that desirable. Why not have it handy for them on your shelves? More and more customers are buying Brooks... making it America's No. 1 seller among tangy catsups. This customer loyalty can add to your profits.

Brooks Finer Foods also include:

THE G. S. SUPPIGER CO. • ST. LOUIS 6, MO.

Brooks came up with a recipe for a tangy "catsup" that gained a large following. Although the packaging is different, it's a variation on the ketchup still purchased today.

Ask any bean counter to calculate how much ketchup was consumed on Route 66 since its inception and they would probably tell you "a heck of a lot." Maybe the amount of tomato puree would even be enough to pave the highway from Chicago to Los Angeles—many times over. For good or ill, Americans love ketchup, the go-to condiment for burgers, hot dogs, French fries, and more.

In the mid–twentieth century, the movers and ketchup bottle shakers of Collinsville, Illinois, recognized this love affair with the red sauce and, in its honor, erected a larger-than-life monument befitting its stature. What is officially known as "the World's Largest Catsup Bottle" (and trademarked as such) now stands as a prime example of roadside Americana on Route 159, just south of downtown. And make no mistake: this bottle is big, measuring in at an impressive 170 feet tall!

The story of the famed ketchup bottle begins in 1891 when local businessmen raised a stake of $5,000 to build what was initially called the Collinsville Canning and Packing Company. In 1907, brothers Everett and Elgin Brooks assumed ownership and ran the place as the Triumph Catsup and Pickle Company. They produced a full line of edible products, including chili beans, spaghetti, hominy, soups, and other canned and bottled goods. But it was the ketchup they sold under their brand name Brooks that sold best. Believe it or not, it was once America's bestselling ketchup.

American Cone and Pretzel took over the plant in 1920, and G. S. Suppiger grabbed the reigns in 1933. Both kept the original brand alive for a good reason: what was originally called Brooks Tabasco Flavored Ketchup was preferred by Saint Louis consumers two to one over all other brands combined. Of course, the McIlhenny Tabasco Company wasn't thrilled with the name and threatened a lawsuit. Seems McIlhenny had copyrighted "Tabasco," so the Suppigers simplified, renaming their moneymaker "Brooks Old Original Catsup."

In 1947, the plant needed a reliable supply of pressurized water for their new sprinkler system, and that's when the idea for the ketchup bottle came to life. Company president Suppiger wanted a hundred-thousand-gallon water tower that would mimic the distinctive tapered silhouette of the company's

The Brooks water tower and adjoining buildings are currently for sale. The new owners get the big catsup bottle water tower and a number of oversized warehouses.

famous ketchup bottles. By 1949, his vision was reality, built on site by the W. E. Caldwell Company of Louisville, Kentucky.

The moneymaking ketchup continued well into the 1950s until Brooks Foods merged with the P. J. Ritter Company. In 1960, the Suppiger family cashed out, and all ketchup-making moved to Indiana. The remaining buildings were used as warehouses until 1993, when Brooks parent company Curtice-Burns, Inc., sold the operation yet again, and the sweet smell of pureed tomatoes wafting through town became but a memory.

At the time, they offered to deed the ketchup bottle water tower to the city of Collinsville, but the town declined, citing the high costs of painting and maintaining it. Enter the Catsup Bottle Preservation Group, a local concern that stepped in to save the tower. They mounted a nationwide campaign called "Paint It!" The goal was to give the landmark a fresh coat of paint and structural repairs.

A year later, Larry Eckert of Bethel-Eckert Enterprises bought the plant. His use for the 90,000-square-foot building was housing commissary goods that his company shipped to military bases in the Midwest. He proved a good caretaker and watched over the monument's two paint jobs—the first organized by the preservation group in 1995 and the second in 2009. But his business downsized, and in 2014, the Collinsville bottle once again had a "For Sale" sign in front of it.

Now, anyone who can afford to pay the bargain basement price of $500,000 can own a piece of American roadside nostalgia, a bona fide classic that was accepted onto the National Register of Historic Places in 2002. "For $500,000, you get the catsup bottle and the warehouse," Eckert was quoted as saying in the *St. Louis Post-Dispatch*. "I'm hoping that whoever buys it loves the bottle and respects its history."

Whether that happens or not remains to be seen since the site comes with no federal funds for upkeep. Any new owner will have the option to keep the water tower intact or tear it down. For the endless miles of highway that are paved with ketchup memories and all the diehard fans who harbor a hankering for the tangy, the tearing-down option would be the target for a handful of rotten tomatoes for sure.

ABOVE: In 1995, the Catsup Bottle Preservation Group saved this landmark roadside attraction from demolition and beautifully restored it to its original appearance.

OPPOSITE: The World's Largest Catsup Bottle stands proudly next to Route 159, just south of downtown Collinsville, Illinois. This 170-foot-tall water tower was built in 1949 by the W. E. Caldwell Company.

2.
THE COZY DOG DRIVE IN

SPRINGFIELD, ILLINOIS

An image of two hot dogs caught in a loving embrace became the eatery's famous logo, an image that was created by Virginia Waldmire, wife of founder Ed Waldmire.

The lowly corn dog is sometimes regarded as a second-class fast food, fighting for rank near the bottom of the roadside food chain. After all, the idea of cooking a hot dog inside a corn muffin is pretty . . . unorthodox. The corn dog is a fast-food freak, an oddity that vendors serve only at state fairs.

But that line of thinking is uninformed. When made correctly, the corn dog is perhaps the perfect marriage of two ingredients, the serendipitous union of a frankfurter and a sweet batter, fried to a golden brown. Its best feature, however, is its sheer portability, like a meat lollipop served with its own holder.

But who should get the most credit for popularizing the corn dog? It's a point of some contention. Evidence can be traced back as far as 1929, the year the Albert Pick L. Barth wholesale catalog of hotel and restaurant supplies featured a "Krusty Korn Dog" baker machine. Other historians credit Carl and Neil Fletcher, who introduced what they called "Corny Dogs" at the Texas State Fair sometime between 1938 and 1942. Still others point to vendors at the Minnesota State Fair who introduced a version they called "Pronto Pups" sometime in 1941.

However, the most widely known account comes directly from the annals of America's Main Street. In Springfield, Illinois, the Cozy

Dog Drive In claims that it was the first to serve corn dogs on sticks, circa 1946. According to accounts, it was restaurant founder Ed Waldmire who perfected the item.

The story begins during Waldmire's college years, when he visited an eatery in Muskogee, Oklahoma. There, he happened to try a new variation of the hot dog that caught his attention. Unlike normal dogs that are either grilled or steamed in water and cradled in a soft bun, this dog came served as an integrated package. That is, the wiener and the bread, made from a corn muffin mix, were fused together to create a tasty amalgam.

Local residents and Route 66 tourists still have an appreciation for the Cozy Dog, despite the increasing competition from many of the other fast-food sources.

Waldmire liked what he saw (and tasted), but after observing the way the proprietors prepared it, he knew that there had to be a faster and simpler way to do it. Waldmire later shared this story with fellow student Don Strand and then headed off to serve in the Army Air Corps. He didn't give his idea any more thought until five years later when he heard back from Strand, whose father worked as a professional baker.

Strand reported that he never stopped thinking about Waldmire's idea and had good news. He claimed that he and his father had concocted a new batter that solved the many issues involved with making a corn dog. His special batter was a perfect consistency, and it clung directly to the uncooked dog after dipping. Plus, it only took a few minutes to cook once dropped into a deep fryer.

Strand sent a batch of the mix to Waldmire, who immediately sequestered himself in his military kitchen to make a batch for testing. He didn't have the proper wooden sticks to skewer the dogs with, so he used cocktail forks. Within minutes, the golden-brown corn dog he had envisioned for so many years emerged from the fryer. Hungry officers were his first test audience, and the corn dogs quickly gained a loyal following at the USO club and the base PX. Waldmire called them "Crusty Curs," and with his wife, Virginia, at his side, he continued selling them at the Illinois State Fair after his honorable discharge in 1946.

Virginia thought the name was adequate for the military market but that a more appealing one was needed for the general public. The

couple began to brainstorm and eventually settled on "Cozy Dog." Around the same time, Virginia came up with the whimsical logo of two hot dogs caught in a loving embrace. The image clicked with the name.

After the couple opened a stand next to their house, travelers on Route 66 went nuts for Cozy Dogs. A second hut followed, and later they moved to another location that shared space with a Dairy Queen. In 1966, they moved again to a location just north of the original.

Today, the birthplace of the corn dog continues to thrive, family owned and operated since 1950. Those stopping off can try the famous Cozy Dog and get an eyeful of cool Route 66 memorabilia. The current generation has adorned the diner interior with a variety of mementos from the historical highway, complete with an onsite gift shop for diehard fans looking for Cozy Dog souvenirs.

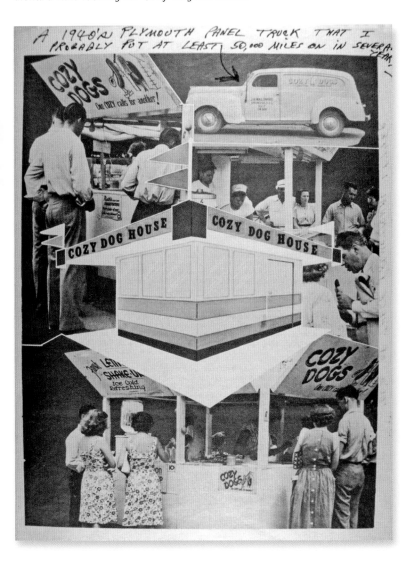

LEFT: Getting the word out was hard work, and Ed Waldmire put some fifty thousand miles on a Plymouth van that he used to promote the Cozy Dogs during the 1950s.

OPPOSITE TOP: In 1949, the Cozy Dog Drive In was born and built on "Route 66" South Sixth Street. Here, the late artist and Route 66 personality Ed Waldmire's van is parked out in the lot.

OPPOSITE BOTTOM: Featuring Formica table tops and typical diner-style stools, the Cozy Dog Drive In allows you to eat inside, order to go, or cruise up to a drive-up window.

3.
WAYLAN'S KU-KU BURGER

MIAMI, OKLAHOMA

The original Ku-Ku building was designed to look like a cuckoo clock, complete with a winged critter of the same name popping out from its hidden nest when the hour struck.

If you're headed down old Route 66 anywhere near Miami, Oklahoma, make it a point to stop off and give Waylan's Ku-Ku Burger some love. Those who try it end up raving about the food as much as the nostalgic atmosphere. People may have an adverse attitude about fast food, but when it comes to Waylan's Ku-Ku Burger, they know that 915 North Main is an address where they can find the beef.

Few people know that at one time Ku-Ku Burger was a relatively good-sized chain of diner-style eateries throughout the Midwest. By some accounts, the chain boasted as many as two hundred locations at its peak. Unfortunately, competition from big chains such as McDonald's and Burger King caused a gradual demise of the operation. Today, only Waylan's Ku-Ku Burger remains.

The Miami location was built in 1965 to catch the attention of motorists zooming by on Highway 66. The chain's original architect designed the front of the building façade to look like an oversized cuckoo clock, complete with a round clock face and hands. Beneath the roof gable, a big yellow Ku-Ku bird sporting a bright orange beak and a white chef's hat welcomes customers with its outstretched wings.

	W CHEESE		SMALL	LRG		KIDS	SMALL	MED	LRG	XLG
GIANT HAMBURGER	2.95	3.25	FRIES	1.29	1.79	DRINKS	1.00	1.19	1.49	1.69	1.99
DBL GIANT HAMBURGER	4.50	5.10	TATOR TOTS	1.29	1.79						
HAMBURGER	1.20	1.45	ONION RINGS	2.09	2.79						
DELUXE HAMBURGER	1.50	1.75	MOZZ CHEESE STIX	2.10	3.20	REAL LIMEADE		1.35	1.69	1.89	2.10
DBL HAMBURGER	1.85	2.35	MUSHROOMS	2.05	3.10	COFFEE	.55		.85		
CORNDOG	1.40		FRIED PICKLE SPEARS	2.05	3.10	HOT CHOCOLATE	.85		1.50		
HOT DOG	1.15	1.40	WAFFLE FRIES		1.75	KUKU WATER	.89				
CHILI DOG	1.39	1.64	KUKU FRIES		3.25	SHAKES		1.69		2.29	
QTR LB HOT DOG	2.29	2.59	KIDS MEAL		3.70	MALTS		1.89		2.59	

COKE · DIET COKE · CAFF-DIET COKE · POWERADE · PEPSI · DIET PEPSI · SPRITE · DIET SPRITE · DR PEPPER · DIET DR PEPPER · MOUNTAIN DEW · ROOT BEER · PINK LEMONADE · ICE TEA

MALTS: VANILLA · CHOCOLATE · STRAWBERRY · CHERRY · PINEAPPLE · RASBERRY · BUTTERSCOTCH · BANANA

QTR LB CHILI DOG	2.59	2.89	COOKIES	.45	3/1.25	doz/4.00	
FRITO PIE		1.85					
BURRITO	1.49	1.74					
BUFFALO BURGER	4.10	4.35					
PORK TENDER SANDWICH	2.99	3.29					
STEAK SANDWICH	3.29	3.59					
FISH SANDWICH	3.29	3.59					
GRILLED CHICKEN BREAST	3.49	3.74					
CHICKEN STRIPS	2.99	4.79					
SHRIMP	5.35						

VANILLA CONE .99 1.25
DIP CONE 1.39 1.69
SUNDAE 1.65
CHOCOLATE · STRAWBERRY · HOT FUDGE · BUTTERSCOTCH · PINEAPPLE
CYCLONE 2.39
YOGURT CONE CHOCOLATE 1.25 1.59
FLAVOR BURST CONE 1.25 1.59

Ask About Monthly Specials

WAYLAN'S HAMBURGERS the Ku·Ku

Although architectural add-ons such as an enclosed glass patio have obscured the original clock face (the top of the dial is still partially visible), one can see that the Ku-Ku is hitting on all eight cylinders when it comes to roadside kitsch.

Eugene Waylan purchased this last remaining Ku-Ku Burger in 1973. Over the years, he worked at various locations and decided that this was the time to get serious about ownership. The hefty roadside sign was slightly modified: where at top center there was once a clock face, Waylan added his name in red neon. Take a careful look at the sign; it's easy to see the plugged holes where the neon used to be.

Other changes followed, and the area got its first drive-thru in 1977 when Waylan installed the equipment needed to serve customers driving up in cars. Now folks traveling down Route 66 had a handy way to grab some grub without adding much extra time to their travels.

Meanwhile, Waylan's Ku-Ku Burger became most famous for its cheeseburger. All its sandwiches are "home-made style" and have a backyard grilled flavor. There are a lot of other tempting menu items too. Some sides are seasonal, so availability depends on the time of year, but you'll never see fried green tomatoes, onion petals, fried pickles and mushrooms, or fried yellow squash on a Wendy's menu.

If you're not a burger lover, there are plenty of other entrees. Waylan's hot dog, chili dog, pork tenderloin sandwich, Frito pie, fish sandwich, shrimp, chicken strips, steak sandwich, Philly steak and cheese, and burrito pack the menu board, completing a sort of fast-food pyramid. Vegans are best advised to dine elsewhere!

TOP: The rear-lit, vacuum-formed plastic counter menu used to be a familiar sight at many fast-food establishments in America, now replaced by flat-panel monitors of various sizes.

ABOVE: The double cheeseburger is the staple American road food, the heavy, heavy fuel required to go the distance when taking the great American road trip to see the USA.

The Ku-Ku is one of the last non-corporate hamburger chain survivors in America. Today, tasteless, bland food threatens to edge out mom-and-pop eateries nationwide.

Although you won't find any beer here, you can still satisfy your thirst for nostalgia with a variety of old-fashioned malts, sundaes, and milkshakes. Anyone who has ever hung out at a small-town drive-in will want to sample the fresh cherry limeade too—a lip-smacking mashup that combines the flavors of two favorites in a single beverage.

While the restaurant is now a highway icon, the man behind the scenes has become a bit of a legend too. Waylan has been flipping burgers there for decades, a job that he reports he loves because he gets a chance to meet people from all around the world. He closes down four times a year on major holidays and takes a sick day only if he has to. If he's not the one manning the grill, he'd rather see his shop closed.

Indeed, when people stop in, they are more than curious to see if Waylan is in the back, toiling over the grill. Some take pictures, and others shake his hand. Everyone leaves happy, pleased to meet the man who helped save this blast from the past. "A lot of things have changed here over the years, but I'm not going to be one of them," Waylan recently told a writer from the *Joplin Globe*. "I don't see myself retiring anytime soon. I'm going to continue to serve here until I can't do it anymore."

ABOVE: Look closely and you will see that the "Waylan's" lettering took the place of a cuckoo clock face. The cuckoo door and clock weights are still in place.

LEFT: Burger and fries heaven at its finest, Waylan's Ku-Ku offers up almost everything the modern-day connoisseur of fast food could hope to order, for less than ten bucks.

4.
HOME OF THE FREE 72-OUNCE STEAK

AMARILLO, TEXAS

No doubt about it, American consumers are all about eating and eating *big*. Since the end of the 1960s, the average portion size of a typical restaurant entree has grown, with restaurants super-sizing everything from soft drinks, burgers, sandwiches, and pizzas to fried chicken, burritos, and barbecue. Year after year, serving plates grow larger as belts are loosened to accommodate expanding waistlines.

Perhaps the best example of this obsession for extreme eating can be found off Interstate 40 in Amarillo, Texas. Here an enterprising Saint Louis transplant by the name of R. J. "Bob" Lee opened a restaurant

The Big Texan suffered a fire in 1976, and $100,000 worth of antiques were destroyed. The eatery was brought back to life with the help of family and friends.

called the Big Texan Steak Ranch in 1960. Supposedly, everything was bigger and better in Texas, and Lee took the stereotype to the extreme, his goal being to open the mother of all steakhouses on the mother of all roads.

Lee made his dream a reality and created a restaurant like no other in the Texas panhandle region. He styled the interior with an eclectic mix of antiques and made sure that only the finest ingredients were used in his kitchen. To satisfy even the biggest boss, the portion sizes were big too.

Many of Lee's customers were true Texans: hungry cowboys always trying to outdo each other with their carnivorous appetites. One Friday, Lee wanted to see how far they would take it, so he pushed together some tables in the dining room and announced a challenge: who could eat the most one-pound steaks in an hour's time? It only cost five bucks, and the top eater could keep the fee.

Much to his surprise, one of the contestants proceeded to gobble down not one but two steaks. The crazy part is that it only took the man ten minutes to clean his plate. But that wasn't the end. According to the legend, he politely requested that a "salad and a shrimp cocktail" be served with his third steak. He ate all of it and then proceeded to devour a fourth steak, along with a baked potato and a bread roll! Even so, he still had room to put away his fifth and final steak.

Lee was dumbfounded and duly impressed by the cowboy's intestinal fortitude. As the crowd went wild with delight, Lee stood on a chair in the middle of the dining room and made the following proclamation: "From this day forward, anyone who can eat an entire 72-ounce dinner in one hour gets it for free!"

And so the "Texan King" was born. Not your typical steak dinner, it is in actuality a monster meal built around a 72-ounce slab of beef

What better way to advertise steaks than with an oversized statue of a steer? At the Big Texan, customers understand that everything is bigger and better in Texas.

grilled to your liking. It also comes with one shrimp cocktail, a baked potato, a salad, and a roll with butter. Not all of Lee's customers were cowboys with bottomless guts, and he figured that the occasional free meal would be well worth the publicity.

He was right on all counts. Through the years, a number of contenders have had their names written into the Big Texan record books. In this regard, truth is stranger than fiction, as the shortest time ever recorded for finishing the Texas King is the one turned in by Molly Schuyler, a competitive eater who weighs in at a diminutive 125 pounds! According to records, Schuyler finished the King in a mere four minutes and fifty-eight seconds.

She decimated the records previously held by Joey Chestnut (8:52) and Frank Pastore (9:30), but her dining skills are even more amazing than that. After eating one complete dinner, Schuyler went on to eat a *second* Texas King meal! In total, she spent fourteen minutes and fifty-seven seconds on both meals. She even went on to beat her own record by forty seconds just a year later.

When it comes to extreme eating and the quest for free food, the Big Texan is a quintessential part of the Route 66 road trip. It's a showcase for folk art, perseverance, and a competitive spirit. Without these things, an American isn't worth his or her salt.

ABOVE LEFT: The Big Texan may be a caricature of what the ultimate Lone Star steakhouse should look like, but it never fails to impress when it comes to the menu.

ABOVE: The Big Texan is known for its excellent cuts of beef and leaves the majority of other nearby eateries in the dust when it comes to New York strip, T-bone, and ribeye steaks.

OPPOSITE: Big Tex has smiled down upon Route 66 travelers for many years now, welcoming visitors to come on in and try their hand at eating a 72-ounce steak dinner (that they get for free if they complete the challenge).

5.
POPS 66 SODA RANCH

ARCADIA, OKLAHOMA

Pops 66 has become a mecca for those addicted to soda pop and the simple comfort road foods that we have all come know and love, most notably the hot dog.

Across America, the debate rages: should a carbonated beverage be referred to as a soft drink or by one of the more colloquial names often given to it? On the East and West coasts, people call fizzy beverages "soda"; in the Midwest, folks call it "pop." Texans and those living south of the Mason-Dixon line use "Coke" to refer to any number of beverages, including Dr Pepper.

Of course, despite the ubiquity of cola when it comes to flavoring nonalcoholic beverages, not all the bubbly drinks consumed in this great land fall under that banner. Like the people who inhabit this nation, diversity reigns supreme in the effervescent world of soft drinks, with today's flavors limited only by one's taste and imagination.

On Route 66 in Arcadia, Oklahoma, Pops 66 Soda Ranch is on a mission to prove this claim. Here, a brightly dressed bartender awaits your order behind a 1950s-style serving bar. But don't corral the kids just yet—he's not serving up anything hard! On the contrary, he's your guide on the journey to soda heaven.

Pops has over *seven hundred* different flavors to choose from, which means that even the pickiest soft-drink aficionado will likely be satisfied. Offerings range from the tried-and-true fruit flavors to old-time standards, such as root beer, ginger ale, and cream soda. But where's the fun in that? Take a walk on the soda pop wild side and try

Avery's Kitty Piddle, Chocolate-Covered Maple Smoked Bacon, or Sioux City Prickly Pear. It's brave new world of flavor.

Outside, Pops has become as iconic as some of the great soda pop bottles from history too. A large metal soda pop sculpture planted directly in front of the building spirals its way into your imagination. Crafted of concentric rings and shaped to hint at the famous Coca-Cola contour bottle, it's a sight to behold and a real roadside marvel when its internal illumination kicks in after dusk. The feeling is "pop" art to the extreme, weighing in at four tons and measuring sixty-six feet in height.

Many Route 66 tourists who stop to see what all the fizz is about learn that the Pops name isn't a reference to soda at all (once upon a time, it was the distinctive sound that the first bottles made when their ball stoppers were opened). Instead, it's a real-life tribute to owner Aubrey McClendon's father, whom he actually called "Pops."

An Oklahoma gas magnate, McClendon commissioned the famous Elliot and Associates architectural company of Oklahoma to come up with the design of the Pops building and bottle sculpture. Devoid of the typical lettering that one might see adorning a commercial structure, the building is unlike anything. Stark yet bold, it's not surprising to learn that the structure has won many architectural honors.

The juxtaposition of the bottle with building sets up a strange interplay. At first glance, the focus is upon the giant neon soda sign as the brain attempts to correlate the scale of things. But it doesn't compute. The oversized bottle makes the building look small. Only when you pull in for a closer look do you realize what you are seeing.

Behind the bottle, a monstrous structure awaits, complete with a cantilevered overhang that covers a row of gas pumps, much like you might find

Pops has hundreds of different soda pop flavors to choose from and literally dozens of root beers, including A&W, Avery's Sarsaparilla, Death Valley Sarsaparilla, Zuberfizz, and more!

The Pops soda bottle sign is like a beacon to those traveling on Route 66, tempting anyone and everyone who passes by to stop on in for a refreshing beverage.

at a traditional, old-time service station. This makes a lot of sense, as the commissioner himself was in the gas business, but it is also fitting for the Mother Road in all her expansive, gas-guzzling glory. The structural metaphor is a promise of cleanliness, speed, and efficiency.

At the same time, the angularity of the roof supports and the expansive windows remind one of the early McDonald's fast-food stands with their rakish roofs. Inside, a quirky diner theme welcomes customers with large plastic bubbles that cascade from the ceiling to hover above cafeteria-like tables and chairs.

With its incredible architecture, colorful signage, and flavorful fare of carbonated drinks, Pops 66 Soda Ranch has proven that new enterprises spawned by Highway 66 can become the roadside icons of tomorrow. When traveling the road through Arcadia, Oklahoma, I challenge anyone who is passing by to ignore it—especially if they are thirsty for a can of soda, a bottle of pop, or even a coke.

6.
HATCH CHILES AND THE 66 DINER

ALBUQUERQUE, NEW MEXICO

A milkshake made with real ice cream is the quintessential diner beverage and one of the items you will be happy to find on the pages of the 66 Diner menu.

Developed on the East Coast, the diner is an American eatery that features a simple menu. Customers come to order standard comfort foods, such as bacon and eggs, meatloaf, French fries, cheeseburgers, and even the old standby called the "open happy waitress": an open-faced grilled cheese sandwich made with bacon and tomatoes. Up and down the Eastern Seaboard, it's a standard menu.

However, the farther west you head, the more you realize that East Coast diner standards no longer apply. Along America's Main Street, the best-kept secret about "roadside food" is that the cooks who control the kitchens love nothing more than adding entrees of their own invention. Every little town along the way seems to have its own niche, serving up palate-pleasing offerings that feature locally sourced meat, vegetables, spices, and other ingredients.

It begins in the state of Missouri, where you will discover that the hamburger is no longer king. In Springfield, batter-dipped hot dogs on a stick rule the roadside at the Cozy Dog Drive In. Dessert means frozen custard or a "concrete," a thicker, heavenly ice cream treat that, when inverted, defies gravity. In Texas, barbecue stampedes its way onto the pages of the menu, most notably tender beef brisket and sausage. In Arizona, the Navajo taco makes its debut, a fried bread creation that borrows the culinary architecture of a Tex-Mex tostada.

As foods become more interesting, one's palate should be well prepared for the spicy bang to come when you cross into New Mexico. Here, the city of Albuquerque is home of the 66 Diner, a comfort food

flashback to the 1950s that knows how to play to its audience. If you can get past all the poodle skirts and memorabilia, you'll see that an entire section of the menu is dedicated to "New Mexico Favorites."

The 66 diner pays homage to both the Spanish and the American Indians who brought their cooking styles to this region so many centuries ago. Today, the Hatch green chile is the star of the show. These are the varieties of the genus *Capsicum*, locally grown in the nearby Hatch Valley. In an area that stretches along the Rio Grande from the town of Arrey north to Tonuco Mountain and southeast of Hatch, the soil and growing conditions create a chile unparalleled.

Hatch chiles find their way into pretty much everything at the diner, but one dish stands out: the Pileup, its trademark entree. Made with a pile of pan-fried potatoes, chopped bacon, chopped green chiles, two eggs any style, cheddar cheese, and red or green chile sauce slathered over the top, it must be tried. When out-of-state travelers passing through on Route 66 get a mouthful, there are no words to describe their satisfaction.

There are other locally inspired dishes to chow down too, including the always popular Frito pie, a favorite at the state fair. According to zealots, the real Frito pie was invented in 1960 by Teresa Hernandez on a particularly inspired day at the

ABOVE: The 66 Diner is designed in the style of Streamline Moderne, an approach that made buildings appear fast, the perfect complement to the speedy pace of American car culture.

BELOW: Hatch green chiles are a popular New Mexico staple and appear regularly in a variety of local foods, including the diner fare found at the 66 Diner.

Santa Fe F. W. Woolworth. For her toppings, she used red chili con carne with cheddar cheese and onions. The fun part was that she didn't use a bowl! The sliced-open Fritos bag provided a handy serving container.

Huevos rancheros is another regional menu item at the 66 Diner, a popular breakfast dish of eggs served in the same hearty manner as the traditional midmorning meal served on a rural farming operation in Mexico. One serving is enough to tide you over well past the afternoon siesta. Fried eggs are at the center of the dish. Lightly fried corn tortillas provide a base, with a tomato-chile sauce poured over the top. Common accompaniments are Mexican-style rice, refried beans, and avocado slices (or a small bowl of guacamole).

So, if you are a fan of homestyle American diner fare, be sure to plug the coordinates of Albuquerque's 66 Diner into your GPS. If you are coming in from the east or New York City, fuhgeddaboudit! Just relax, squeeze out of your comfort zone, and order one or two of the regional specialties. Your taste buds will thank you.

ABOVE: When the sun goes down, the 66 Diner literally comes alive on the exterior; its sexy curves and swooping neon tubing sear a tasty image directly into your brain.

OPPOSITE: Legally, you can't call yourself a "diner" unless you have a counter with stools, stainless-steel surfaces and fixtures, neon signage, and classic tile work. At the 66, it's all here.

TOP FIVE

WEIRD to go and WEIRD to do

1 2 3 4 5

BEEF BURGER BARREL

3102 Plains Boulevard, Amarillo, Texas

Part of Amarillo since 1947, the Beef Burger Barrel is an unabashed icon of Texas roadside dining and a must-see stop when traveling Route 66. It's one of a kind and the type of roadside kitsch that gets the attention of any admirer of vintage burger joints.

DOG HOUSE DRIVE IN

1216 Central Avenue Southwest, Albuquerque, New Mexico

Everyone raves about the chili at Dog House, with some saying you aren't a true resident of the city unless you eat here. Fans of the TV shows *Breaking Bad* and *Better Call Saul* will recognize this place right off, as it has appeared in several of the shows' episodes.

HENRY'S HOT DOGS

6031 West Ogden Avenue, Cicero, Illinois

Henry's may very well be one of the last surviving relics in the Route 66 town of Cicero. It's the quintessential vintage hot dog joint with a sign that is worth the trip itself. Mmm, Chicago-style hot dogs . . . they sure don't make 'em like this anymore.

BAGDAD CAFE

46548 National Trails Highway, Newberry Springs, California

The famous cafe from the movie of the same name is a remote truck stop cafe run by owner Andrea Pruitt. It's definitely a novelty stop that's worth seeing, especially if you are a fan of the film and like to eat in the typical roadside joints.

ROCK CAFÉ

114 West Main Street, Stroud, Oklahoma

Taking its name from the local sandstone that makes up its exterior, the Rock was started in 1936 by Roy Rieves. Today, it has appeared in many television shows, has its own cookbook, and has gained notoriety worldwide as an icon of historic Highway 66.

WON'T COME BACK FROM DEAD MAN'S CURVE

America's Main Street paints a safe and happy image of a road without danger. Unfortunately, the route was not lacking when it came to automotive hazards. Take a pedal-to-the-metal look at the road segments that earned notorious nicknames such as "Bloody 66" and "Death Alley," where countless motorists bought the farm in horrific head-on collisions and deathtrap accidents long before the days of mandatory seat belt laws and automatic airbags.

1.
TOWANDA'S DEAD MAN'S CURVE

TOWANDA, ILLINOIS

Hardly dangerous by today's high-speed standards, pictured is another life-taking bend in the road, located somewhere along the Oklahoma stretch of old Highway 66.

During the heyday of Route 66 tourism—between the 1940s and 1960s—traveling by automobile was often a matter of life and death. Four distinct factors contributed to this state of affairs: a disregard for safety belts, automotive design, distractions along the shoulder, and the inherent design flaws of America's two-lane highways.

Nothing more than a coffin on wheels, the "modern" motorcar of the mid–twentieth century offered the intrepid motorist little in the way of safety features. Interiors were fabricated of skull-crushing sheet metal and studded with eye-gouging control knobs. Inches from unprotected eyeballs, windshields featured glass that splintered into lethal fragments upon impact.

Car seats lacked a primary restraint system, allowing you to catapult forward after a sudden impact. Rollover protection? There was no such thing, let alone a reinforced roof to keep your neck from snapping if your vehicle flipped over.

At the same time, the nature of Route 66 made it a dangerous driving venue. Unlike the modern superhighway with its nonstop driving lanes, America's Main Street presented numerous chances for the motorist to make a fatal mistake. In the towns Route 66 crossed, inclement weather and road conditions accounted for much of the vehicular mayhem. Frequent stoplights raised the stakes at far too many intersections, as did crosstown traffic comprising local yokels clogging up the roads.

Ineffective warning signs and poor road markings added another level of danger. Worse yet, the glowing raft of neon and flickering chase-lights that festooned the carnival of billboards, restaurants, shops, and other roadside attractions grabbed one's focus away from the road.

By the time American inventor John W. Hetrick registered for the first airbag patent in 1951, Route 66 had already earned nicknames such as "Bloody 66" and "Death Alley." Cemeteries in the eight states along the route overflowed with the mutilated victims of traffic accidents. Like so many horrific clips from a driver's ed shock film, the grisly scenes of bloodied bodies trapped between shards of twisted sheet metal and broken glass replayed along the route day after day, hour upon hour, minute after minute.

While seat belts had been around since the turn of the century, today's three-point design didn't get traction until a few years after Roger Griswold and Hugh DeHaven filed for their patent in 1955. Detroit let the bloodbath on the highways continue until 1959, when Congress finally passed legislation to force American automakers to comply with a list of safety standards. But it was too little, too late for the untold number of victims of 66. The most lethal stretches of the old road had already gained infamy through lurid stories told and retold like so many folktales.

Many parts of 66 were forever ensconced in myth, most notably those exaggerated bends more commonly referred to as "Dead Man's Curve." Rather than spend extra money blasting through a geologic feature, roadbuilders often incorporated wild detours to circumvent the topography. Even under normal driving conditions, these flawed examples of highway engineering offered little reassurance, especially if the visibility was poor and you exceeded the speed limit.

Singers Jan and Dean immortalized one such Sunset Boulevard curve in their iconic pop song "Dead Man's Curve" of the 1960s, but it was Route 66 that laid claim to at least three well-known examples.

ABOVE RIGHT: While pop stars Jan and Dean recorded their song about a particular curve in California, roads all over America had their version of the dangerous hairpin to brag about.

RIGHT: During the 1960s, highway deaths were a big problem in Arizona, leading the *Chicago Tribune* to describe Route 66 as "a vacationland highway where death takes no holiday."

DEATHS ON 66 BIG PROBLEM FOR ARIZONA

Drivers Bring Doom to Themselves

Phoenix, Ariz., Nov. 9 (UP) —Route 66—perhaps the most sung about, talked about, written about United States highway—stretches 381 miles across Arizona taking a bloody toll of weary and unwary travelers.

This year — from January thru September—59 persons died in 35 fatal automobile crashes on the vacationland highway where death takes no holiday.

Don't blame the highway. There are better roads than some sections of highway 66 but thousands upon thousands travel it without accident.

Frustrated authorities say it's tired, sleepy, drinking, reckless, irresponsible drivers that bring death to themselves and others.

TOP: In the Ozark region of Missouri, the Devils Elbow curve was so sharp that after years of horrific automobile accidents, it earned the nickname "Bloody 66."

ABOVE: To slow people down, highway departments put up all sorts of signs and most, like this example along Oklahoma 66, were ignored.

The first is an otherwise uneventful stretch of Historic US Route 66 in Mesita, New Mexico. There, locals duly crowned a 180-degree bend to the left "Dead Man's Curve." The second was in Illinois. Before the stretch of road that ran through Lincoln was gobbled up by Illinois Business Highway 55, the portion that ran near two cemeteries earned the very same name and spawned myriad ghost stories and other creepy tales.

The third and most well-known death curve tricked motorists driving along Route 4 in Towanda, Illinois, to their doom. There, the highway punished drivers hurtling in from Chicago at a high rate of speed. Unfamiliar with the road, these motorists suddenly encountered a 90-degree bend and lost control. Known as the "Full Grown Bears," the State Highway Police of District 6 patrolled this area frequently, clawing the bodies from the pavement on a regular basis.

In one incident, a house situated on the west side of the curve was knocked off its foundation after a semitrailer careened off the road and ran smackdab into it. Much to their chagrin, the homeowners replaced the front porch on a regular basis—tourists passing by on Route 66 just couldn't help but run into it. A guardrail of some design would have saved the day, but the legend of Dead Man's Curve reserves no place for one.

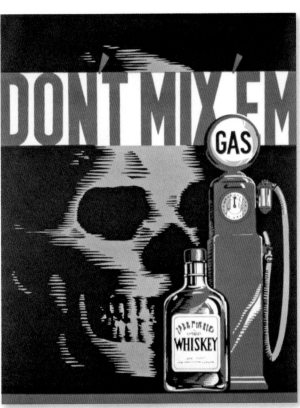

ABOVE: Now marked by sign and placard, the dangerous curve in Towanda, Illinois, is perhaps the most infamous of Route 66 death traps (just 18 feet wide, it barely held one car safely).

LEFT: When you travel Route 66, the thing you least want to do is mix gasoline and whiskey—a potent combination that more often than not leads to vehicular mayhem.

2.
CONQUERING LA BAJADA MESA

SANTA FE, NEW MEXICO

ABOVE: In recent years, La Bajada has been barricaded off, and people are fighting to keep visitors out. The road has crumbled and has become even more dangerous to drive on.

OPPOSITE: A skull was about the only thing that caught the motorist's attention and was used to good effect to warn of the dangers on New Mexico's infamous La Bajada Mesa.

In Santa Fe, New Mexico, the legend of La Bajada Mesa began long before Route 66 or even the contraption known as the horseless carriage. At one time, the high desert mountain was part of the topography traversed by the El Camino Real de Tierra Adentro, a rocky and dangerous path that led up and over it as early as the 1600s.

American Indians who originally occupied the region used the path to travel through the area, as did overland adventurers who had the mettle to trailblaze their way across the Southwest in covered wagons. In 1869, US Army Lieutenant John Bourke described the descent as "so risky that stage passengers always alighted and made their way on foot, while the driver found abundant occupation in taking care of his train and slowly creeping down with a heavy brake on the wheels locked and shod and the conductors at the head of the leaders."

For travelers moving between the Rio Abajo (lower river) and Rio Arriba (upper river) of New Mexico's primary government districts, the El Camino Real was the most direct route. At the time, there were only two other options: follow the Santa Fe River through the canyon of Los Bocas Canyon (the mouth) or go entirely around La Bajada Mesa and come in through the Galisteo Basin. Albeit safer, those options demanded much more travel time.

When the twentieth century arrived, the precarious trail became a bona fide roadway on the way to Santa Fe, and during the period between 1902 and 1926, it was designated New Mexico Highway 1.

Motorists of yesteryear approached driving with a cavalier attitude despite the dangers on the roads and the complete lack of any sort of automobile safety features.

This was part of the National Old Trails Road Highway system, a more extensive network promoted as the "Ocean to Ocean Highway." Ford's Model A had the power to take the hills, though not the safety features to survive an accident.

Years later, when Route 66 was being planned and created, the powers that be went to work finding ways for travelers to make easy-to-follow connections from one end of the route to the other. In 1926, highway officials eyed the rustic New Mexico trail that was absorbed by the state highway system and incorporated it into the Mother Road. At its busiest, estimates show that 1,200 cars clambered over La Bajada Mesa every day!

But the segment was only used by Route 66 until 1932, when highway boosters abandoned it in favor of a much safer path that roadbuilders bulldozed a few miles to the east (near the current interstate). It's no wonder that the segment was temporary. Although it provided a more direct path, La Bajada (the descent) was dangerous. In those days, it had no pavement to speak of, and the design was ill-suited for automobile traffic in two directions, let alone one. The road wound down the face of the hill in a series of twenty-three hairpin turns and dramatic switchbacks.

Along the way, the worst spots were bounded by craggy walls of crumbling basalt rock on one side and precarious drops on the other, with only the occasional retaining wall. In the span of just three-quarters of a mile, the road descended 1,500 feet! At the southwest edge of the mesa, the volcanic escarpment that makes up the foundation towers six hundred feet above the desert floor.

Despite the danger, people driving Route 66 came in droves, pulled by the directness, the scenery, and the American Indian attractions. At one time, corn dances were held at the very top of the mesa, something that tourists of the day just couldn't get enough of. Although the distance between Albuquerque and Santa Fe was only sixty-four miles, it took six hours to make the drive if one included La Bajada Mesa!

La Bajada Hill, between Albuquerque and Santa Fe, New Mexico

Typically, the corn dances ended at dusk, setting up quite the predicament for motorists ill-prepared for night driving. During the 1910s and 1920s, this made for an extremely challenging and dangerous ride home, especially since the vehicles of the day didn't have the robust headlamps needed to make it back down the winding road in the dark.

The road at La Bajada Mesa had a 28-degree slope, which was quite difficult to maneuver even during the day. Anecdotes reveal that travelers were quite inventive in their efforts to make their way over the descent. According to accounts, some motorists even improvised handheld torches to help light their way to the bottom of the hill, hoping to generate enough illumination so they could navigate their way around the dangerous corners rather than drive over the edge and slide into oblivion.

The switchbacks at La Bajada may have looked tame from a distance, but once you were driving on them with four wheels, it was another story completely.

3.
PASADENA'S SUICIDE BRIDGE

PASADENA, CALIFORNIA

Along California Route 66, Pasadena's infamous Arroyo Seco bridge had every right to be called majestic, yet it was plagued with case after case of people leaping from it to their deaths

In October 1929, the American stock market crashed, marking the beginning of the Great Depression. Suddenly, desperate measures became the norm. Many Americans faced the hard times with determination, digging their way out one day at a time.

Unfortunately, not everyone had the mettle to face the challenges of the age—especially if they were flat-out broke and lost everything they owned. For some, suicide even became a viable option. Tall buildings and monuments became popular destinations for people seeking to take their last swan dive into oblivion. In America, one of the more popular suicide destinations gained prominence along the old Route 66 in California. The Colorado Street Bridge in Pasadena was a graceful concrete arch design that earned itself the macabre moniker "the Suicide Bridge."

In 1912, the construction of the bridge came in at $191,000 ($4.5 million adjusted for today), and sponsors hoped it would be a jewel in the city's crown, drawing people with its ornate structure and unusual curved roadbed.

Much to their chagrin, a dark shroud enveloped the bridge's reputation even before workers finished construction, when an

accident caused a worker to plummet to his death. According to some sources, he landed in wet cement below, and no one retrieved the body. To maintain schedule, work continued, and the worker was forever entombed in the cold, hard concrete.

After the bridge was completed, despondent laid-off workers and others began tossing themselves over the side. The first recorded suicide on the bridge took place in November 1919, and over the years, more copycats followed. The epidemic reached a morbid crescendo in the six years between 1933 and 1939, during which time fifty individuals leaped to their deaths from the elevated roadway.

Perhaps the most bizarre of these tragedies involved Myrtle Ward and her young daughter, Jean. Apparently, Myrtle despaired after she lost her job at the local cafeteria. She saw no way to remedy the situation and make things better for her family, so on May 1, 1937, while her husband was away at his temp job, she took little Jean to the bridge. Ignoring the witnesses who tried to stop her, she picked up her three-year-old daughter, tossed her over the side, and leaped to her own death.

Also known as the Colorado Street Bridge, the structure is almost church-like in its grandeur, complete with grand arches and intricate architectural detailing.

Oddly, the bridge had other plans for Jean Ward. Witnesses heard her crying for her mother from the stones and brush below and quickly came to her rescue. What they found stunned even the most jaded: whether it was divine intervention or just dumb luck, Jean had somehow managed to survive the fall without injury, the only person known to plunge from the 143-foot-high bridge and live to tell about it.

To date, the bridge has claimed the lives of more than one hundred fifty people. While jumping deaths have somewhat slowed (a suicide barrier has been erected), many claim those lost at this site live on. Of course, Myrtle Ward and the unfortunate worker are regular bridge ghosts, but more spirits haunt the structure.

Supposedly, people who care to cross the span on foot can hear the cries of the dead as they walk across. Over the decades, witnesses have recounted stories about a man who wears wire-rimmed glasses; he routinely waltzes back and forth across the bridge's roadway and then vanishes before the eyes of onlookers. Multiple accounts describe the antics of a white-robed woman also seen on the bridge playing out her last moments before leaping to her death.

Given its architectural grace and grandiose views, it's a shame that the Colorado Street Bridge has earned such a gloomy reputation. For those heading west to the road's terminus, it's a part of life and history that must be accepted. On this segment of old Route 66, the ghosts just happen to come with the scenery.

ABOVE: From beneath, the dramatic architecture of the Pasadena bridge traversing the Arroyo Seco Canyon seems almost holy in the diffused lighting of the late afternoon.

OPPOSITE: At night, the bridge in Pasadena takes on an almost Gothic appearance; fluted columns topped by globe lamps illuminate a rigid, steel-railed roadway meant to keep cars in.

4.

ATOMIC BOMB ROAD BUILDING

MOJAVE DESERT, CALIFORNIA

MODEL OF PROJECT

CARRYALL

Project Carryall engineers went so far as to construct scale models of what they believed the land would look like after a few well-placed atomic bombs were exploded.

During the 1960s, America's great idea men huddled in secret bunkers across the country and devised grandiose schemes to make our lives better. According to their predictions, we would soon travel back and forth to Mars, use picture phones to communicate with friends and family, and strap on personal jetpacks to ease the morning commute, achieving better living through technology.

A large part of these promises featured a genie that we had recently unleashed: nuclear power. Atomic energy would soon power our planes, trains, and automobiles, and America would ride into the next century on a wave of free energy. At the same time, visionaries proposed that the atom bomb could be used as a tool, harnessed for good. By way of its power, large-scale engineering projects such as canals, harbors, and roads could be constructed in a fraction of the time and at a fraction of the cost.

The process of scraping the earth with shovels, bulldozers, and heavy equipment seemed ridiculous in comparison. Look how long it took to construct Route 66 and pave it from end to end. Why not take a nuclear device, place it accordingly, and blast away the earth to create a clear and viable pathway for the roads and highways to come?

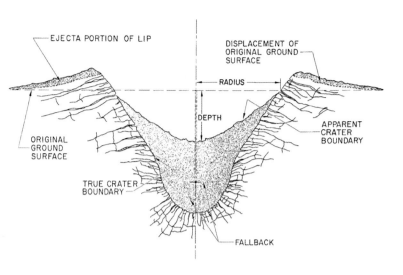

EJECTA PORTION OF LIP

DISPLACEMENT OF
ORIGINAL GROUND
SURFACE

RADIUS

DEPTH

ORIGINAL
GROUND
SURFACE

APPARENT
CRATER
BOUNDARY

TRUE CRATER
BOUNDARY

FALLBACK

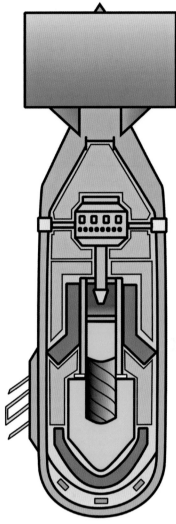

It sounds like a ludicrous plan, but it was seriously studied by road builders in the 1960s. Since the dawn of the motor age, road builders faced many obstacles when they tried to take on terrain of any major altitude. Mountains meant using dynamite to blast paths for dangerous switchbacks. There was no practical way to burrow a straight and even path through solid earth unless you dug an expensive and dangerous tunnel.

Out in the Mojave Desert of California, the Bristol Mountains were a prime example. When Santa Fe Railway first laid tracks in this area, engineers scoffed at the notion of going over the mountains since it was much easier and cheaper just to detour around them. Later, when Route 66 was being planned, designers faced the same issue of getting over a four-thousand-foot hunk of solid rock.

Of course, the Santa Fe Railway wasn't satisfied with the extended detour. There had to be a way to make a straighter and flatter path through the mountains, but they didn't really want to invest the money that it would take to do it. After engineers did some studies, they came back with the bad news that the proposed route would require a two-mile tunnel or excavations into the rock, some five hundred feet in depth. The railroad had deep pockets, but not *that* deep.

Only the government had that kind of money to waste, and that's just who stepped in to continue the ill-fated plan. At the time, the Atomic Energy Commission was looking for peacetime uses for "nuclear devices." Route 66 was being phased out, and California was beginning construction on Interstate 40, its multilane replacement. Why not use hydrogen (fusion) and atomic (fission) bombs to blast through the mountains?

ABOVE LEFT: The scientists who came up with the idea of atomic bomb road building had everything mapped out, including a cross-section of what the bomb's aftermath would look like.

ABOVE: Little Boy was the first atomic bomb to be dropped on Japan on August 6, 1945. It's doubtful that anyone at the time predicted its potential use in building large-scale engineering projects.

TOP: Developed by Scottish road builder John Louden McAdam, the Macadam method was a way of compacting material to make smooth surface, the standard for decades.

ABOVE: The 1962 "Sedan" plowshare test displaced some 12 million tons of earth and created a crater that was 320 feet (100 meters) deep and 1,280 feet (390 meters) wide.

ABOVE RIGHT: The proposed construction of a roadway through the Arizona mountains was documented with a map published in "Engineering with Nuclear Explosives," a government publication.

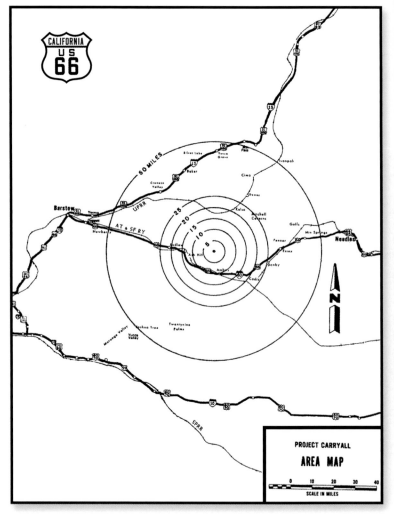

This was the thinking of Project Carryall, a boondoggle that wasted $770 million dollars over a fifteen-year span studying how to use nukes to build American infrastructure. Their suggestion to the California State Division of Highways? Instead of using conventional explosives and large earthmovers, place a couple dozen atom bombs in a strategically staged array and proceed to blow the holy hell out of the Bristol range.

All it would take to blow the passage through the mountain was an arsenal of twenty-three bombs! One of these bombs would be reserved for the creation of a giant crater, a catch-basin that would trap rainwater and storm runoff.

Engineers estimated that the bombs would displace some 68 million cubic yards of dirt (which still had to be scooped up and trucked away to who knows where since it would most likely be highly

As part of Project Plowshare, a program to develop peaceful applications for nuclear explosives, the Lawrence Radiation Laboratory at Livermore conducted Project Dugout on June 24, 1964.

radioactive). Government bean counters gave their nod of approval, citing the cut-rate cost of $13.8 million ($8 million cheaper than if they used standard methods).

"The study group has concluded that this project is technically feasible," wrote a California highway engineer. "It can be done, and it can be done safely." But they were wrong: there was no way to contain the fallout, as proven by the 1962 test creation of the Sedan Crater in Nevada, and the radiation would make any blast site uninhabitable.

In 1977, the operation came to a close, and all they had to show for the effort were a few craters. The final analysis was that while building roads with nuclear devices was a good idea *in theory*, it was a terrible idea in practice. In the long run, digging out roads the old-fashioned way was much healthier for animals, children, and other living things.

5.
SWITCHBACKS OF SITGREAVES PASS

OATMAN, ARIZONA

West of Kingman, Arizona, the so-called hairpin turn was one of the most treacherous features of the Arizona Gold Road (named so because of mining operations) heading west.

When Route 66 was in its infancy, taking a trip cross-country was not a relaxing experience. First, there were far fewer amenities than one might see along today's roadside. There was no such thing as calling AAA to have someone come out and tow you to the nearest facility. If you broke down, you had to rely on your mechanical abilities to get going again.

In the Midwest, rambling from town to town along the old road wasn't that much of a challenge, because the odds were in your favor against breaking down too far from the next settlement. But the stakes were much higher in Texas, New Mexico, and Arizona, where large expanses of country meant that you had to drive for days to get across state lines.

Out west, the conditions were a lot tougher. In addition to the grueling distances, the heat played a significant factor in stranding vehicles. If you pushed your motor to the extreme, your reward would be a blown head or a seized engine (not easily repaired in the boonies). But if they planned and carried an ample supply of water, even neophytes had a good chance of going the distance.

Of course, all bets were off when it came to crossing steep mountain grades or other treacherous inclines. This was primarily the case in Arizona, just west of once-bustling goldmining town Oatman. Here, the pre-1952 alignment of Route 66 meandered up and over the dramatic terrain of Sitgreaves Pass and offered motorists a real-life rollercoaster thrill long before theme parks were commonplace.

Located in the Black Mountains of Arizona's Mohave County, Sitgreaves Pass is essentially a gap between the mountains rising to 3,586 feet in elevation. Here, in 1857, famous trailblazer and explorer Edward Fitzgerald Beale completed what was called Beale's Wagon Road. To honor one of his men, he named it John Howell's Pass (it's believed that Howell met his maker building this pioneering trail). When Lieutenant Joseph Christmas of the Corps of Topographical Engineers passed through on a survey mission in 1858, he renamed the pass to honor one of *his* fellow explorers, Captain Lorenzo Sitgreaves.

Back in the day, travelers motoring west to California approached the pass with a fair amount of fear and trepidation. Rich or poor, Model T or Duesenberg, it didn't matter: the twisted path put everyone's car to the test. Here, Murphy's Law seemed to rule, and if there was any mechanical fault in your engine, you could be sure something would snap or blow out just about one-quarter of the way up the hill.

Standing above the mining town of Goldroad and looking west toward the Colorado River Valley, hopefuls got an eyeful of the "road" that awaited. Here, carved into the light-brown earth of the stark desert mountains, the two-lane road resembles a wild snake, tamed to follow the treacherous path through the craggy terrain. Rising and falling with every contour of the land, the endless switchbacks, hairpin turns, and steep grades were a white-knuckle challenge for even the most experienced.

Strangely enough, many of the motorists who made the trip in underpowered vehicles often tackled the grade by going at it backward. Driving in reverse gear offered more torque! This strange trick also solved the possibility of your engine stalling out on the steep slopes, because many of the gravity-fed fuel systems of the age were inadequate when it came to conditions of extreme incline.

Back in the days before AAA and twenty-four-hour wrecking services, running off the road on treacherous stretches of Route 66 meant that your journey was over.

ABOVE: By the time you reached the highest elevation across the Sitgreaves Pass, you were at 3,550 feet above sea level. Good thing your oil and transmission fluid were topped off.

RIGHT: A horseshoe curve near Kingman, Arizona, provides a shaded spot for an traveler of an earlier age to stop and admire the scenery along 66.

Horse-shoe Curve on National Highway "66", near Kingman, Arizona

Occasionally, drivers came along who had no intention of piloting their car up and over the pass. How did they get to the other side? As the legend goes, locals often staged teams of horses nearby and offered their services to pull Model Ts up to the summit (presumably, it was easier to get down than up). At the same time, one or two wrecking companies got in on the act too, cheerfully pulling the fearful flatlander's car up and over the pass in exchange for a few dollar bills.

Today, the Oatman Road approach has been superseded by the Yucca bypass (following the rail line), although it's still an option for the daring who wish to experience it for themselves. As one of the forgotten and most dangerous segments of the old Route 66 Highway, Sitgreaves Pass is an ideal place to see Arizona, New Mexico, and Arizona in one fantastic vista—and remains a proving ground to test one's mettle behind the wheel.

With its hairpin turns and dangerous switchbacks, the Gold Road near Oatman, Arizona, proved to be a formidable obstacle for many people heading west.

6.
THE ROAD WITH MANY MONIKERS

MAIN STREET AMERICA, USA

Route 66 was designated as a historic highway by many of the states it passed through, including California. Signs were erected to boast of the road's new status.

What's in a name? Plenty . . . if you're talking about the highway called Route 66. Too expansive, too prosperous, too gregarious, too enjoyable, too historical, and too notorious to be satisfied with a single moniker, the "old road" is well-deserving of its numerous titles. Each reveals a different part of the road's personality and character.

"Highway 66" is officially part of the United States Numbered Highway System, a set of routes typically referred to as US routes. The American Association of State Highway and Transportation Officials are responsible for the route numbers and the locations, and they follow these simple rules:

1. All routes that follow a north-south alignment are odd numbered. If one of these federal routes is a major conduit, it's designated with a number ending in 1. The lowest numbers begin in the east; the highest numbers are in the west.

2. All routes that move traffic east-west are even numbered, with the major roadways ending in 0.

3. Last, but not least, all highways numbered with three digits are spur routes of parent highways, although they may not even be connected.

But Highway 66 was far too impersonal a title for a roadway of this stature. During its heyday—when the traffic was heavy and towns prospered—promoters nicknamed it the "Main Street of America." In the same way that the main street of a small town is the hub of that community, 66 ties multiple states together with a sense of community. Route 66 is a destination in its own right: the cities and attractions that give it life are the equivalent of the hardware stores, five-and-dimes, drugstores, and barbershops that once thrived along main street.

While the entire stretch of road may be considered historic, there are certain segments of old Route 66 that are better preserved than others.

But travel twenty years into the past and you will see that the experiences along Route 66 were not so pleasurable. During the years of the Great Depression—from 1929 and on—many people didn't have enough money for the necessities, much less extra cash for leisure travel. These were dark days on America's Main Street, known by far too many as "the Road of Flight."

Down-and-out Americans packed up their Ford Model As with as many household goods as the springs could hold and pointed their wheels toward the West Coast. Far from the ravaging dust storms and failing crops, there had to be a better life at the end of the highway's rainbow. The point of convergence for this great migration was Route 66. As with a great river, most smaller tributaries led directly to it. If you were in a motorcar and heading west, there was a good chance that Route 66 would be a part of your journey.

Although many people saw 66 as the grand matriarch of travel, some viewed it with more frivolity. One of these people was American humorist, writer, and actor Will Rogers, who cut his eyeteeth on Route 66, rambling about many of the small towns during his younger days. A Cherokee from Oologah, Oklahoma, he became the most widely read newspaper writer of the mid-1920s and penned entertaining articles for the "common man" laden with good-natured humor and sage advice.

ABOVE: In Albuquerque, New Mexico, the historic Aztec Motel promotes its location by referring to 66 as the Mother Road, a popular nickname for the Chicago to Los Angeles highway.

By 1933, Rogers was a household name and the top male box-office draw in the United States. He became honorary mayor of Beverly Hills, California, and years later, the US 66 Highway Association bestowed him with a great honor: Route 66 would be co-named the Will Rogers Highway. Today, enthusiasts can learn more about him at the Will Rogers Memorial Museum in Claremore, Oklahoma, a fitting tribute to the man who once said, "I never met a man I didn't like."

Yes, Highway 66 has many names. But whether you call it the Will Rogers Highway, the Mother Road, the Main Street of America, the Road of Flight, or even the official designation, Highway 66, one thing is sure: "Historic Route 66" is a highway that has risen from the ashes of near obliteration to meet the promise of restoration.

LEFT: Heading west from Del Rio, motorists know that they are driving on a historic highway, courtesy of the highway department commemorative signage.

OPPOSITE: When Route 66 was decommissioned in 1985, many of the states took down the familiar Route 66 signs and suddenly it was as if the road never existed.

TOP FIVE

WEIRD

to go and

WEIRD

to do

1 2 3 4 5

CUCAMONGA SERVICE STATION

9670 Foothill Boulevard, Rancho Cucamonga, California

A hundred-year-old gas station along Route 66, the Cucamonga Service Station is a historic site, now welcoming visitors as a museum. Route 66 Inland Empire California Association (IECA) embarked on an ambitious journey to renovate and rebuild the gas station to make it look like it did during its heyday.

DICK'S TOWING SERVICE

911 North Broadway Street, Joliet, Illinois

This whimsical dedication to American road travel is located right next to Dick's actual towing business. With just the simple placement of a few old cars and some signage, Dick's has become yet another modern-day landmark of Route 66 sought out by roadway adventurers.

STANDARD OIL GAS STATION

South West Street, Odell, Illinois

A 1932 Standard Oil service station restored to its former glory, Odell's is open seasonally but well worth the visit. The restoration by the Illinois Route 66 Preservation Committee is award winning, complete with visible register gas pumps and period signage.

PETRIFIED FOREST NATIONAL PARK

Route 66, Northeastern Arizona

Arizona's Petrified Forest National Park is filled with trees fossilized into colorful hues of stone. Like the Grand Canyon and other natural wonders, it should be one of the top must-see sights on anyone's Route 66 bucket list. Be sure to see the petroglyphs of Newspaper Rock.

HISTORIC SELIGMAN SUNDRIES

22405 Historic Route 66, Seligman, Arizona

Historic Seligman Sundries is yet another convenience store turned junk-a-torium and selfie stop poised oh so elegantly along the old Mother Road. It's all here, folks, including the tail end of an airplane, a vintage black-and-white police cruiser, gas pumps, folk art, and crazy signs.

INDEX

Note: Page numbers in **bold** refer to figures.

About the Author

A member of the American Society of Journalists and Authors and of the Authors Guild, Michael Karl Witzel is an award-winning writer, photographer, and artist living in Austin, Texas.

He is the author and photographer of over two dozen books about American pop culture, including the award-winning *The American Gas Station: History and Folklore of the Gas Station in American Car Culture, The American Drive-In, The American Diner, The American Motel, Route 66 Remembered, Legendary Route 66: A Journey Through Time Along America's Mother Road, Barbecue Road Trip*, and many more.

His writing and photography has been published in *Texas Highways, Motorhome, The Fort Worth Star-Telegram, Mobilia, Check The Oil!, Rider Magazine, Route 66*, the *Society for Commercial Archeology Journal, Invention & Technology*, and *Volkswagen World*.

Photo Credits